IMAGES
of America

ASHEVILLE *and* WESTERN NORTH CAROLINA *in* WORLD WAR II

Johnny F. Ray served in the army during World War II. (Augusto Brisco Ray Collection, Liston B. Ramsey Center for Regional Studies, Mars Hill College.)

ON THE COVER: The National Gallery of Art opened on March 17, 1941, only nine short months before the bombing of Pearl Harbor. The directors of the museum were worried about what the Axis powers might do to these national treasures if they gained a foothold on U.S. soil, so they moved pieces to the Biltmore Estate. (National Gallery of Art, Washington, D.C., Gallery Archives.)

IMAGES
of America

ASHEVILLE *and* WESTERN NORTH CAROLINA *in* WORLD WAR II

Reid Chapman and Deborah Miles

ARCADIA
PUBLISHING

ISBN 978-0-7385-4342-0

Published by Arcadia Publishing
Charleston, South Carolina

Printed in the United States of America

Library of Congress Catalog Card Number: 2006928936

For all general information contact Arcadia Publishing at:
Telephone 843-853-2070
Fax 843-853-0044
E-mail sales@arcadiapublishing.com
For customer service and orders:
Toll-Free 1-888-313-2665

Visit us on the Internet at www.arcadiapublishing.com

The authors, together with the Center for Diversity Education, wish to thank the veterans, civilians, and survivors who shared their stories. Their service and sacrifice is their greatest legacy. This book is dedicated to them.

Contents

FOREWORD

The 20th century's two world wars framed the early years of my life and molded the rest of it. We believed the First World War was the "War to End All Wars." The Second World War taught me that we must always work for peace.

I was born just after World War I, surrounded by a culture of war. My father, uncles, and their friends all volunteered in "the Great War." In our house, we children treasured trophies such as a German helmet and an Iron Cross. My brother and I dressed up in World War I uniforms from our grandmother's attic. We pored over a picture book of the war: ruined towns, blasted cathedrals, long lines of captured troops.

Then came the Great Depression. There was an ominous undertone to the news in the 1930s: unrest in Europe and a strident new militarism in Germany. We saw German troops goose-stepping and saluting Hitler; we saw the large Krups guns swinging into battle position—and shuddered.

Along with these events, two seminal occurrences took place in my life: I began studying Latin, which I loved, and I saw the movie *All Quiet on the Western Front*. My seventh-grade companion and I clung to each other, sobbing "Why? How?" I then committed myself to working for peace: I would specialize in foreign languages, preparing myself for a career as a diplomat promoting world peace.

In 1942, I graduated from college with a Spanish degree and was recruited to work for the Army Signal Corps. I learned code breaking and translating. I felt a sense of urgency, of working for the Right Cause. I believed that contributing to the war effort was hastening the peace.

Again I was in a culture of war. I married a navy pilot and agonized when he went to Europe. His brother was killed, as were cousins and friends. When my husband returned from the war, we both vowed to work for peace all our lives. When our children asked their father for war stories, he said there was nothing glamorous about wars, that they were brutal and generally unnecessary.

Our family has been active in international programs. They have been in the Peace Corps, the UN, the Diplomatic Service; they have lived and worked in foreign countries. When the Friendship Force was being established in North Carolina, Governor Hunt asked me to organize a Western North Carolina chapter. President Clinton appointed me to several international conferences, where I promoted peace. I continue to oppose war and violence by working through the political system for positive, peaceful outcomes.

I applaud the Center for Diversity Education's work. Through your efforts, people can be taught to respect and cooperate with each other.

—Marie Colton
North Carolina General Assembly's
First Female Speaker Pro Tempore

Acknowledgments

The work of archivists is critical to the work of historians. This book owes a large debt of gratitude to their dedication and patience. The authors would like to give heartfelt thanks to the following: Helen Wykle and Jamie Patterson of the Special Collections at University of North Carolina at Asheville's Ramsey Library, Ann Wright and Zoe Rhine at the North Carolina desk of Asheville's Pack Memorial Library, Diana Sanderson at Warren Wilson College and the Asheville School, Jeff Futch at the North Carolina Department of Cultural Resources Western Office for sharing his contacts, Sion Harrington and Kim Cumber at the North Carolina State Archives, Jill Jones at the Swannanoa Valley Museum, Cassie Robinson and Peggy Harmon at the Liston B. Ramsey Center for Regional Studies at Mars Hill College, Jeff and Hyman Dave at Dave Steel, Murat Yazan at Henderson County Library, Marcie Thompson at Transylvania County Library, Patrick Willis at the Canton Area Historical Museum, Helen Rice for her information on Sayles Bleachery, and George Frizzell at Western Carolina University's Hunter Library. Thanks also go to Mandy Carter, Mark Burdette, and Erika Grosser, who worked on the center's archives, and to the Janirve Foundation for the funding needed to complete the archive. We would also like to thank those who have donated to these archives over the years and to encourage future gifts; these contributions have made projects like this possible. Unless otherwise indicated, photographs are from the Center for Diversity Education's archives.

Many volunteers worked with the Center for Diversity Education to interview veterans and civilians and to catalog their stories and pictures; our appreciation goes out to them and to the board of directors, who enthusiastically support the organization's mission.

Reid Chapman thanks his wife, Cathy Cleary, who for months shared the dining room and the dinner table with stacked boxes of interview transcripts, release papers, and drafts of the book. She long ago earned his love but now deserves thanks for her support and patience. He would also like to thank Marc Archambault for his careful reading of the text and his gentle suggestions for making it better.

Deborah Miles sends her love and deep gratitude to her husband, Marc Rudow, for teaching her about commas and for calling to say it's time to come home for supper; to her sons, Josh, Caleb, and David, for reminding her to turn off the news and listen to the music; and to her family, John, JoAnn, John II, and Rebekah Miles, for teaching her to remember and tell the stories of the ancestors.

INTRODUCTION

It was the greatest honor of my life—to serve my country. —Charles McAdams

War is not glamorous. War is and always has been about killing and death. —Henry Colton

I did nothing heroic—each of us just did what we had to do. —Landon Robert

A government does not tell me who my enemies are. —Michael Robinson

This is only the second time I have told this story—once to my grandson when he was bored on a long car trip and now here. —George Lamprinakos

I was anxious. For three years I never knew if I was a bride or a widow. —Mary Ellen Wolcott

Each individual's experiences prior to, during, and after the war have shaped how they interpret this history. Charles McAdams grew up in segregated Asheville and served in both the segregated and later the integrated army. Henry Colton felt more acutely the pain of losing his brother than the pride of being a decorated pilot. Landon Roberts, whose father sat on the Madison County draft board, parlayed the steadiness needed for Pacific service into a successful legal career. Rabbi Michael Robinson, horrified by what he saw in combat, became devoted to peace and reconciliation. George Lamprinakos, who as an 18-year-old infantryman pushed across the frozen landscape of Europe, held these memories within himself. Mary Ellen Wolcott threw herself into her work as a reporter and into organizing other war wives before her husband returned safely to her arms. These experiences, and many more, indicate the breadth of participation in this conflict.

This book does not attempt to be exhaustive of the contributions of Western North Carolina to World War II. Rather it seeks to shed light on the myriad ways the World War II generation contributed to a common goal of defeating fascism, what was learned along the way, and what their experiences can teach the generations of today and tomorrow. The global economic crisis of the 1920s and 1930s leads to a discussion of xenophobia, racism, gender roles, scapegoating, anti-Semitism, and genocide—all issues that are still, all too tragically, a part of the contemporary experience. As many interviewees expressed, we need to seek different solutions to conflict.

The call to arms in 1941 centered on the dangers of dictatorship and the promise of democracy. It asked Americans to sacrifice not only to defend their way of life at home, but to extend to others the same promise of freedom. The process laid bare some inconsistencies in the social and political life of the United States. World War II led to a reexamination of our democratic society. Cultural conversion does not happen easily, but this all-consuming conflagration wrought such transformations. In the face of calamity, Americans willingly risked change.

Some of the changes happened suddenly and dramatically. The U.S. Armed Forces learned to adapt rapidly, changing battlefield tactics and behind-the-scenes strategic planning in response to their successes and failures. The late Robert Morgan saw this as a pilot with the Eighth Air Force, which rather than mimic the Britons' unsuccessful nighttime bombing missions, engaged in a daytime campaign. Although this led to an 80 percent loss of flight crews to death or capture, it proved much more effective in destroying targets. Eventually these airmen learned to lessen their losses by flying in tight formations. Morgan explained, "The formation was so tight that at times I had a point man to keep their wing over our wing with about five feet between us in height." Another veteran cited as the greatest attribute the United States' use of interdisciplinary teams in which all members had input. This innovation allowed a team to see problems from a variety of perspectives, greatly increasing its ability to solve problems. Such is the great strength of a working democracy: recognition of all perspectives. This flexibility in restructuring traditional methods gave U.S. forces an upper hand over the enemy.

Other changes came about painfully slowly but have fundamentally altered the fabric of American society. Hendersonville's George Gash remembered the treatment of African American soldiers: "Sometimes our worst enemies in Europe were our own troops. If we went to a bar or something, some white soldiers, especially if they were from the Deep South, expected it to be the way it was back home. But things we did here did not go over there. The worst experience I had was in Louisiana. There the white soldiers told the German prisoners of war we were guarding that they did not have to follow our orders because we were black. . . . I thought, 'Why fight? If I am not good enough, why fight?' "

African Americans were generally assigned jobs involving manual labor. They dug ditches and carried heavy timbers with the engineers, difficult work made more perilous due to the risk of being shot or shelled. They loaded ammunition into ships for the navy and fuel onto trucks for the army. Delivering supplies, often truckloads of filled gas cans, overland to the troops was necessary, but extremely dangerous, work. This task was assigned to an outfit known as the Red Ball Express. African American troops did 80 percent of this job, driving days with no sleep and often facing enemy fire. Charles McAdams of Asheville described it as "no pleasure trip. We had a job to do and we did it." Black troops valiantly served the nation but by the end of the war demanded better treatment.

Race was not the only civil rights issue that began a slow but irreversible turn in World War II. During the war, women stepped into jobs previously closed to them. They drove trucks, flew airplanes, and supervised men. Prior to the war, women accounted for 20 percent of the work force. That figure grew to 34 percent during the war years, but only half those remained at war's end, as returning soldiers resumed their positions. The military, due to the great need, also opened its ranks to women. Black Mountain's Bertha Moore, a recent graduate from Johns Hopkins at the time, joined the army as a nurse. She was initially classified a private—quite an insult given her level of training. Moore eventually received an officer's commission and the resulting pay increase. Over time, the military and society at large has come to better appreciate, and reward, the contributions of women.

Major political change happened in the hours after Japan bombed Pearl Harbor. World War II marked an end to American isolationism. Prior to the First World War, Europe, Africa, or Asia's problems were of little concern to the United States. After the signing of the Versailles Treaty, complacency to world problems again beset this nation. Many politicians, including North Carolina's own Sen. Robert Rice Reynolds, held staunch isolationist views. World War II reversed decades of policy. For the next 60 years, the United States would not idly watch foreign hostilities. This government came to recognize that other nations' policies impact it just as U.S. actions affect others.

This book seeks to put a very human face on these huge cultural shifts, helping readers see how world history and personal history intersect, how both change together. Beginning in the early 1900s, the American eugenics movement argued for the superiority of the white, Christian race. This pseudo-science bolstered the social and legal stature of Jim Crow laws in the South and was an inspiration to Adolf Hitler and the followers of the Nazi Party. The genocidal premeditation of the Nazis shocked the Allied forces. An estimated 11 million Jews, Roma, people with disabilities, and others were systematically murdered. Over 250,000 survived the slave and death camps. One of those survivors, Markus Reich, escaped a death march from Auschwitz and later was a witness at the war crimes tribunals. By 1951, he was living at the Asheville YMCA and eating at the downtown S&W Cafeteria, where he could communicate what he wanted by pointing. Reich willingly faced the hardships of immigration for a new beginning and a better life. His story echoes the entire world coming to grips with the violent need to destroy fascism and to come face to face with its own history to create a new beginning and better lives.

Veterans, civilians, and survivors all over the world simply wanted to pick up where they had left off before the war began. Soldiers used the networks the war had created to find jobs, for emotional support, for camaraderie. Even today, veterans' groups host reunions for a dwindling number of participants. The American Field Service (AFS) ambulance drivers' network created the AFS student exchange program to promote peace, one such group that used its connections to bring about transformation.

Some lasting changes had more negative consequences. Armament contractors used networks forged with the government during the war to continue to fuel U.S. economic prosperity. It was the designer of D-Day, Pres. Dwight Eisenhower, who in 1961 cautioned about this very transition: "In the councils of government, we must guard against the acquisition of unwarranted influence, whether sought or unsought, by the military-industrial complex. . . . Only an alert and knowledgeable citizenry can compel the proper meshing of the huge industrial and military machinery of defense with our peaceful methods and goals so that security and liberty may prosper together."

Every citizen of the world owes his or her freedom and security to this entire generation. These men and women fought against the idea that a human or groups of humans were created superior or inferior. Now it is in the hands of the generations that follow to reach across the lines that divide people to bridge peace and economic well-being "so that security and liberty may prosper together."

Haywood Street in downtown Asheville remained active throughout the war, as indicated from this 1940s photograph. (Pack Memorial Library.)

One

Before the War

The economic, social, and political climate of Western North Carolina (WNC) on the eve of World War II can be described briefly: poor, segregated, and isolationist. Within months of the bombing of Pearl Harbor, these categorizations would be challenged.

Farmers in greater WNC had suffered for years prior to 1929; the Great Depression did not change their lives much. Families who were able to hold on to their land simply continued to grow what they needed or made do without. Asheville, however, entered the Great Depression in a textbook manner: boom then bust. The city borrowed millions of dollars in the 1920s to build the infrastructure necessary to sustain the expanding private development. The stock market crash dealt a nearly fatal blow to Asheville's economy.

Germany suffered under an even greater debt. To galvanize their power, the German government began to institutionalize the hatred of certain people, culminating in the Nuremberg Laws of 1935. These laws drastically limited the lives of Jews. Many decided to leave as they saw the climate worsening; some emigrated to WNC, enhancing the social fabric of our region.

Racial segregation also characterized the South, with dramatically inferior facilities available to African Americans. Jim Crow laws and customs drew a color line between the white and black communities in the same ways the Nuremberg laws did in Germany. All schools and eating facilities in WNC, in addition to hospitals, movie theaters, and most occupations, were clearly delineated for white or colored people exclusively.

One of North Carolina's senators during this time was Asheville native Robert Reynolds, a Democrat who took a staunch anti-alien position with comments like, "America must be saved for Americans." He also held a hard-line isolationist stand. He favored withholding aid to France and Britain until those nations repaid their debt from the First World War. Indeed he consistently opposed the Lend-Lease Act until 1941. Meanwhile he advocated closer ties to Germany. These policies often put him in conflict with President Roosevelt.

On December 7, 1941, the isolationism and poverty of this region ended. Segregation, however, took longer to shake off.

Asheville in the 1920s was a boomtown. A nation of high-rollers vacationed in brand-new hotels and resorts, enjoying the scenic beauty of the mountains. Kenilworth, Beverly Hills, Malvern Hills, and Norwood Park housing developments flourished during these years. This fueled local real estate speculation, with prices escalating with no apparent end in sight. A brochure dating from the 1920s entitled *Live and Invest in the Land of Sky* noted, "Asheville Realtors are proud to repeat the statement that 'No one has ever lost money by investment in Asheville real estate.' For it's true!" To support such development, the city built infrastructure, such as the Douglas Ellington–designed Lee Edwards High School (now Asheville High), pictured here. (Ball Collection, Ramsey Library, UNCA.)

West Asheville's neighborhoods, including developer J. T. Horney's Horney Heights, were largely built during this time. In 1927, J. T. Bledsoe, another area developer, built the Bledsoe Building, part of the commercial anchor in downtown West Asheville. A deed of trust was issued on the Bledsoe Building in 1928 for $65,000; it sold in 1931 for $45,000 and again in 1944 for $35,000. (Ball Collection, Ramsey Library, UNCA.)

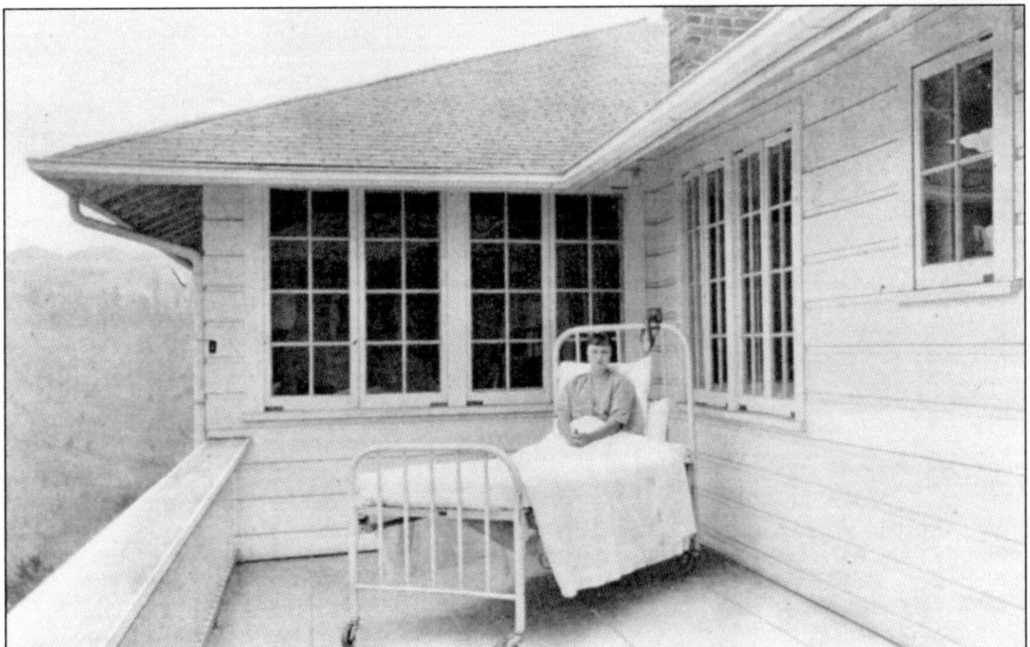

Tuberculosis treatment centers, where patients could benefit from fresh air, were prevalent in the 1920s. Asheville was among the leading cities for this remedy, playing into the real estate boom by creating an excess of hospitals and TB sanitariums. (Pack Memorial Library.)

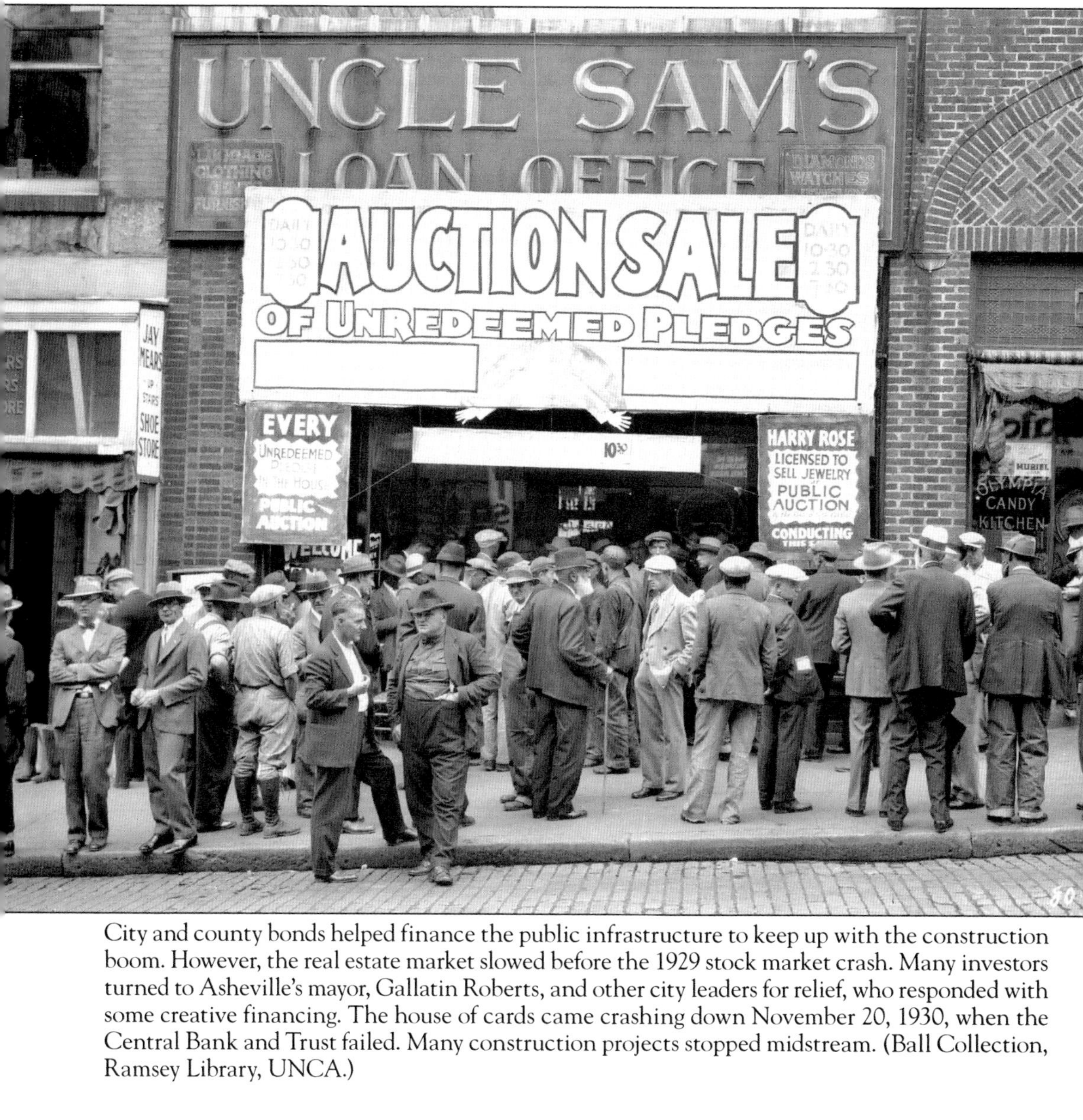

City and county bonds helped finance the public infrastructure to keep up with the construction boom. However, the real estate market slowed before the 1929 stock market crash. Many investors turned to Asheville's mayor, Gallatin Roberts, and other city leaders for relief, who responded with some creative financing. The house of cards came crashing down November 20, 1930, when the Central Bank and Trust failed. Many construction projects stopped midstream. (Ball Collection, Ramsey Library, UNCA.)

Like a hangover after a hard night of drinking, the 1930s reminded Ashevillians of the excesses of the previous decade, marked by speculative real estate investment and a boomtown economy. On February 23, 1931, Roberts (top, left) publicly disgraced and having resigned as mayor, shot himself in a bathroom in the Legal Building (at right) after being indicted by a Buncombe County grand jury of misuse of public funds, among other charges. (Top, Pack Memorial Library; Bottom, Ball Collection, Ramsey Library, UNCA.)

Western North Carolina saw the same economic stagnation that much of the nation felt in the 1930s. However, the region's natural beauty created an opportunity for Civilian Conservation Corps projects. Many undertakings, such as the Blue Ridge Parkway, kept WNC working. (Blue Ridge Parkway Archives.)

The American eugenics movement bolstered the beliefs of the Ku Klux Klan for white Christian superiority. The leadership was an integral part of Buncombe County government and often participated in downtown Asheville parades, as seen in this 1925 photograph. (Herbert Pelton, photographer, Pack Memorial Library.)

In Asheville, William Pelley founded a racist and anti-Semitic hate group known as "The Silver Shirts." They marched in local parades down Patton Avenue and distributed their national weekly newspaper from offices next to the train depot in Biltmore Village. According to an arrest warrant put out by Sheriff Laurence Brown, Pelley (below) was wanted for "making fraudulent representation . . . engaging in, among other things, un-American activities." By the early 1940s, the organization became defunct after Pelley was convicted of tax evasion by the IRS and sent to prison. (Top, Pack Memorial Library; Bottom, Ball Collection, Ramsey Library, UNCA.)

Pelley's

"The Silvershirt Weekly"

his world contains thousands of men eager to launch movements that save society, but the urge that secretly motivates most of them is a childish itch to open the mail

OLUME 1 | Asheville, N. C., October 3, 1934. | NUMBER 6

Does the Jew Face Disaster?

If the Jew is at any time in danger of destruction from the "barbarians" about him, it is because he has stupidly provoked such destruction by his insolence and ethics. As for race hatred having been eliminated in Russia, ask a Russian and not a Jew.

THESE are the days when the Jews among us are beginning to fear for themselves with a fear that is gigantic. This fear ever seeks expression in self-assurances about Security. A people who do not fear for themselves are unmindful about security. They do not think about it the clock around.

Consider Rabbi Isaac Stollman, reported in The Detroit Jewish Chronicle as saying: "The Jew must understand that he is alone in a great roaring sea where every wave is eager to swallow him, and he is at all times in danger of destruction from the barbarians surrounding him."

In speaking of Russia, the Jew George Galvani says: "The elimination of race hatred is without doubt the great accomplishment in all history."

THE SILVERSHIRTS have suddenly come upon the American scene with certain prescriptions for society's convalescence. They and their leaders have perceived in the ethics and strategies of the megalomaniacal Jew, a menace to the social peace and welfare which cannot be removed until a whole nation takes cognizance of this radical and revolutionary faction in its midst and permanently "binds" it so that honest men can function. Within another year the entire United States will have awakened to the fact that the Jewish Problem takes precedence over all other problems begging public attention.

The Jews themselves are aware of this. They strive to meet it by a Fear-warning issued to their own people on the one hand, and a whistling-in-the-dark about elimination of race hatred in Jewish Russia on the other.

They fool no one but themselves.

If, therefore, the Jewish Question is the biggest question in the nation in the days just ahead, it is time for Silvershirts to examine with the constructive research of true statesmen just what they are confronting in Judah as a problem, what the fullness or emptiness of Israel may be as of present moment, what the Jew is in essence—and in later issues, just how he shall be dealt with, to establish society again on the basis of wholesomeness, sanity, prosperity and tranquility.

We as a people are confronting great Days. But we as Silvershirts have done begging issues. We propose to look into the malfeasance of the times, among Gentile as well as Jew, and order our houses and cleanse our own temples.

"If such research be Jewbaiting, then let us make the

Bauhaus design was a burgeoning artistic movement in Germany in the 1920s. Many "traditionalists" objected to this new approach for design, and eventually the Nazi Party outlawed this artistic movement, labeling it "degenerative art." Many Bauhaus artists fled to the United States, among them painter Josef and weaver Anni Albers (seen here *c.* 1936), who came to WNC to work at Black Mountain College. This photograph was taken by Ted Dreier. (Josef and Anni Albers Foundation.)

Before 1938, cigarette paper was produced exclusively in Europe. As war loomed, this greatly concerned tobacco companies. Harry Straus, a German immigrant, worked with engineers on a water process to make such paper. With $2 million in backing from cigarette companies, he set up Ecusta in Brevard, North Carolina, employing over 900 people by 1947. Cigarettes were a part of every weekly supply packet during World War II.

Gus Lichtenfels, a Jewish immigrant from Germany, came to Asheville in 1914, married Asheville native Edna Long (above, left), and operated the Asheville Cotton Mill on River Road (below). Hitler's Nazi Party led Germany to pass the Nuremburg Laws in 1935, restricting Jews from jobs, schools, and public places. The Lichtenfelses received letters from relatives, who feared the worse was yet to come, pleading that he sign an affidavit so they might immigrate to America. They eventually helped over 30 friends and family members escape. Their son Joseph recalled, "My Mother, Edna, and my sister, Helen, had a large file drawer where they kept all the [carbon copy] forms that had to be filled out for each person. . . . Senator Robert Reynolds was very helpful in helping us get so many family members out." (Top and bottom, Ball Collection, Ramsey Library, UNCA.)

While in her hometown of Leipzig, Germany, Hilde Cohen cared for a group of children whose refugee parents had disappeared following a Nazi pogrom. After the war, she married Fred Hoffman, whose family had been rescued by the Lichtenfels family.

The economic mood in most of Western North Carolina had lifted by the late 1930s, as evidenced by these photographs of Canton's 1939 Labor Day fair. Canton's Champion Paper Mill kept employing folks throughout the Great Depression. The problems of Europe seemed far distant to most of the region's populace. The greatest concern to this crowd might have been the troubled teens portrayed in the film *The Angels Wash their Faces*, starring Ronald Reagan, as advertised on the marquee of the Colonial Theater (lower photograph). (Top and bottom, Canton Area Historical Museum.)

Asheville native Sen. Robert Reynolds was a staunch isolationist right up to the bombing of Pearl Harbor. For political expediency, he often embraced Roosevelt's policies, though he was among the few dissenting votes on the Lend-Lease Act of 1941. Despite his unpopular beliefs (and due largely to seniority policies within the senate), Reynolds held the key position of the chair of the Military Affairs Committee during the war. (Pack Memorial Library.)

Pres. Franklin Roosevelt came to Asheville for the dedication of the Great Smoky Mountains National Park in 1940. Senator Reynolds rode out to the park with Roosevelt and in Roosevelt's dedication speech suffered ribbing regarding his isolationism. (Grove Park Inn Historical Collection.)

Two

HOMEFRONT

As soon as the reality of Pearl Harbor set in, young men and women began to enlist. Others waited for their draft notices. Alan Neilson and Lucille Roberts were teenagers at Grace High School when they fell in love. Neilson decided to wait for his draft notice, allowing a few more months to hold the hand of his future wife.

Asheville inductees left for boot camp from the Asheville City Hall parking lot. Julia Ray recalls that they left in segregated fashion—whites one day, blacks another. Photographer Baker Barber captured a similar moment in Hendersonville (viewable online at http://www.henderson.lib.nc.us/bakerbarber.htm). In the photograph, soldiers and their families stood in front of the bus station where the Red Cross set up two coffee stands. A rope was placed between the two tables with blacks on one side and whites on the other.

At the advent of war, WNC caught the attention of the federal government, bringing about economic gain. According to local historian Lou Harshaw, the topographically isolated location close to Washington, D.C., along with its overstocked housing market, built during the real estate boom of the 1920s, created the perfect location for armed service administration. The government filled up the inns, businesses, and residences, replacing tourists with a civilian and military workforce.

The region's few factories put local citizens to work with military contracts. Other private organizations found that by renting space to the government, they could gain much needed capital. Montreat's Assembly Inn "cleared" $75,000 during the six months they leased their facility to the federal government for the Japanese and German internment camp—enough to pay off all their debt, put in sidewalks, and establish a substantial capital account. While the war provided an opportunity for some in the region to profit, the loss of students proved quite a drain to local colleges.

The nation's mood quickly changed on December 7, 1941. Asheville's Vernon Branson (left) was on the USS *Tennessee* at Pearl Harbor that Sunday morning. Branson was in the mess hall when he heard planes overhead. He stepped outside in time to see one of the hangers erupt in a huge ball of flames. He was ordered to his battle station, but it quickly became apparent that Branson's broadside gun would not be effective against the low-flying attack aircraft. He was ordered below to load ammunition. He spent the next 24 hours three decks below the waterline. "The air inside our compartment became so fouled with oily smoke [see below] from the burning *Arizona* and the *West Virginia* that we were ordered to put on gas masks. It was so dark we could not see the ammunition we were loading but did it all by feel." (Bottom, Library of Congress.)

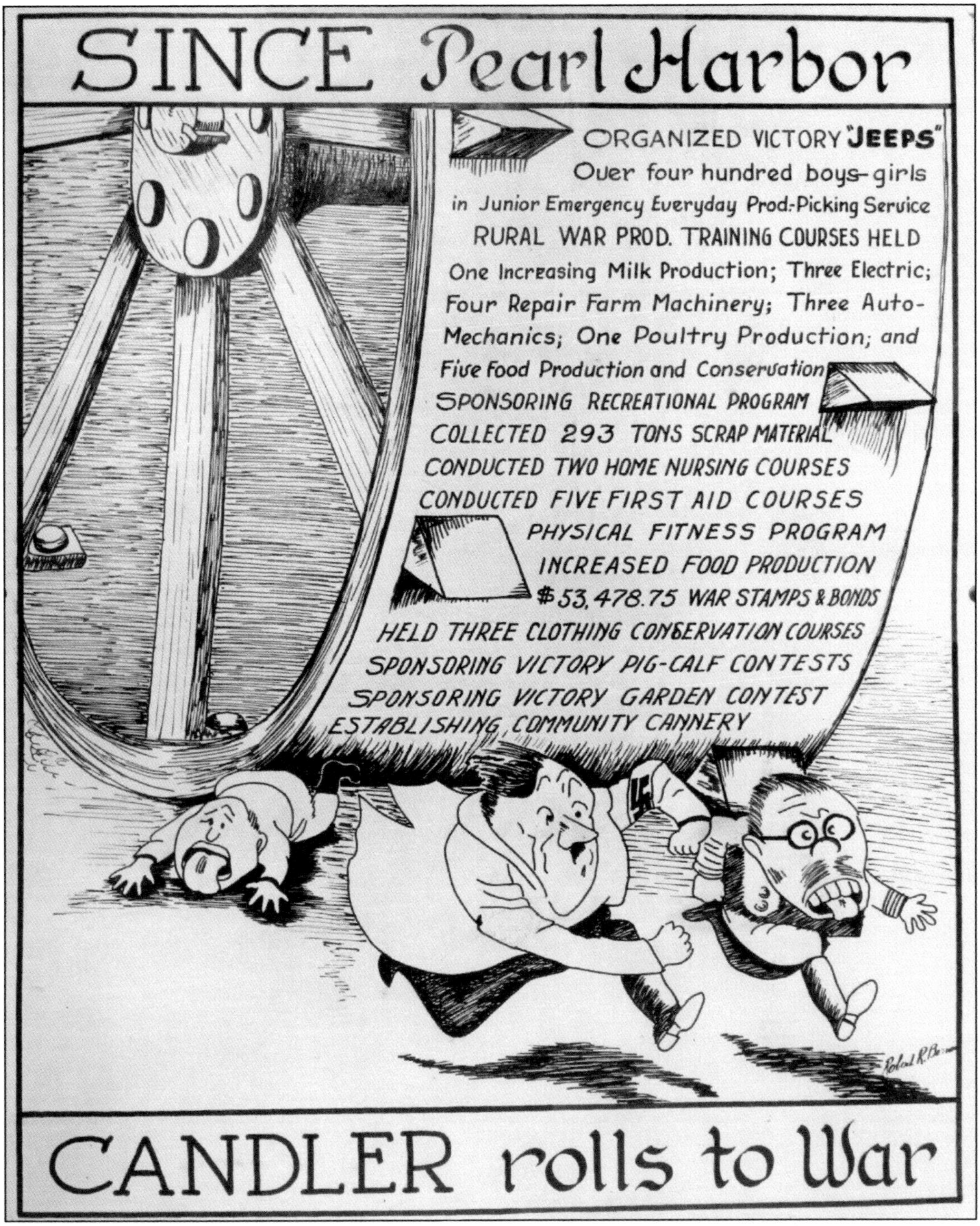

The bombing of Pearl Harbor mobilized Americans. This poster documents the ways in which the Candler community helped in the war effort. (James G. K. McClure Collection, Appalachian Archives, Mars Hill College.)

For six months in 1942, the Assembly Inn at Montreat, North Carolina, became home to 264 Japanese and German civilians, 152 of them children. These non-combatant enemies were mostly the families of businessmen who were taken into custody by the Immigration and Naturalization Service when the United States entered the war. The German men (top, playing chess) were allowed to stay with their families, while the INS soon sent the Japanese men to an internment camp in Texas. The lower picture shows U.S. State Department representative Elmer Fisk with two Japanese internees. (Both photographs E. B. Bowers, photographer, Presbyterian Historical Society, Presbyterian Church (USA) Philadelphia, Pennsylvania.)

The Germans lived on one floor, while the Japanese lived on another. Only rarely were the two groups allowed to interact, as indicated in this picture of German children playing. The Assembly Inn, a service of the Presbyterian Church, sought to treat these internees in the most humane way possible. The staff, including desk clerk Elizabeth Barr Bowers (who took these photographs), showed a great interest in the families. (E. B. Bowers, photographer, Presbyterian Historical Society, Presbyterian Church (USA) Philadelphia, Pennsylvania.)

The federal government set up the offices of the Postal Accounts Division of the post office in the Grove Arcade (above) during the war. Retail and office tenants received one month's notice to vacate the premises. This building housed the federal government for the next 55 years. (Ball Collection, Ramsey Library, UNCA.)

The federal government rented out three of Asheville's central hotels and the basement of the City Auditorium for the Army Redistribution Station (ARS), where soldiers returning from overseas received their next orders. The Battery Park Hotel on Haywood Street (right) housed the headquarters on its mezzanine level and a club for enlisted soldiers on its roof. Golf and tennis were available free of charge at the Grove Park Inn. Soldiers reported to the basement of City Auditorium. Here they would be given maps of Asheville, including directions on proper etiquette to display while a guest in town. The Vanderbilt Hotel contained the chaplain's office on the ground floor, where soldiers could find Catholic, Protestant, and Jewish clergy. The Asheville Biltmore (below) also housed soldiers. (Top and bottom, Pack Memorial Library.)

From May 3, 1943, until January 7, 1946, the Weather Wing of the Flight Control Command, later known as the Army Air Forces Weather Service, called Asheville home. Its offices were located on four floors of the City Building (left). The U.S. Army was trying to spread out its headquarters in case of an attack on Washington, D.C. According to Lt. Gen. William O. Senter (bottom), then commander of the Weather Wing, in a 2002 interview, "I went down to Asheville . . . and rented that seven-story building on the spot. . . . I took half of it and [Army Airways Communications System] took over the other half. . . . They were just trying to get everybody out of Washington." (Left, North Carolina State Archives; Bottom, Air Force Weather History Office.)

The Weather Wing's staff (some of whom are pictured at top at the officer's club) initially consisted of 72 officers and 60 enlisted men from all over the United States. The unmarried soldiers found rooms at the Asheville Apartments on Market Street, while many of the officers moved their families here and bought houses. In 1944, the Weather Wing hosted a weather officer conference in Asheville (lower picture). With Asheville City Hall rented out to the federal government, the city leaders made a deal to put their offices in the Buncombe County Courthouse. (Bottom, Air Force Weather History Office.)

A convoy of soldiers heads down Brevard's Main Street on February 19, 1941. A number of women reported that when troop convoys were coming through Asheville, students from Lee Edwards High School would stand on the street and wave on the soldiers. GIs often threw out slips of paper printed with their names and post numbers. Many of the young women would write to these men throughout the war, even though they really had never previously met. (Top and bottom, Austin Collection, Transylvania County Library.)

The National Gallery of Art opened on March 17, 1941, only nine short months before the bombing of Pearl Harbor. The directors of the museum were worried about what the Axis powers might do to these national treasures if they gained a foothold on U.S. soil. Local historian Lou Harshaw, a college student at the time, recalls seeing the boxes while visiting her family friends the Cecils at the Biltmore House: "These big, heavy crates were stacked almost to the ceiling with a little tiny walkway in between. You had to almost turn sideways to get through. They had all the windows blocked off. Though it was not important to me at the time, years later I understood the significance. They were the National Gallery pictures, stored there in case of bombing." (Top and bottom, National Gallery of Art, Washington, D.C., Gallery Archives.)

GROVE PARK INN

above ASHEVILLE, N.C.

. . . For the Duration

It is with a mixture of regret and pride that we advise you that Grove Park Inn will be taken over by the United States Army on August 19, for the duration of the war and for six months thereafter.

We deeply regret the necessity of cancelling all reservations as of that date. We regret too, that for the duration we will not have the privilege of entertaining the many friends of the Inn who have been coming here regularly for years.

However, you will be glad to know that the Inn will be used as a rest center for officers and men of the Army who have been wounded in action. Here, in the bracing mountain air they will store up renewed health and vigor before returning to the battle areas.

We know you will understand our feeling of pride that the Inn will be privileged to play such an important role in the winning of the war.

And when Victory is won, and we receive our "Honorable Discharge" we will be happy to once again welcome you to Grove Park Inn—a *New* Grove Park Inn with added recreation facilities and new, luxurious comforts for your enjoyment.

Until then, we remain,

Yours for an early Victory,

Burt Frei
Manager

In 1942, the State Department leased the Grove Park Inn (top), temporarily housing 242 German, Italian, and Japanese diplomats. Guards were placed at all entrances, and barbed wire was strung on the perimeter of the property. Alan Neilson, age 16 at the time, worked as an elevator operator at the Grove Park Inn. He remembers seeing the laundry of the diplomats and families, including diapers and all manner of clothing items, strung from one end of the Great Hall to the other. During this time, the inn did not accept any other guests. The hotel mailed this letter of apology (bottom) to guests whose reservations were necessarily canceled. (Top, Pack Memorial Library; Bottom, Grove Park Inn Historical Collection.)

Following the permanent placement or return of diplomats, the inn was used first by the navy and then by the army as a site for "Rest and Relaxation" (R and R) for returning soldiers and then officers. (Grove Park Inn Historical Collection.)

The Philippine government in exile, led by Pres. Manuel Quezon (right), had its headquarters at the Grove Park Inn for three months in 1944. (Library of Congress.)

The cannon seen here (in front of the Vance Monument) was captured from the Germans in November 1918 and mounted at Pack Square to memorialize World War I soldiers. In a gesture of defiance, it was taken to the Asheville Hide and Metal Company to be recycled into new weapons against Germany. The holding ring from the cannon remains attached to the base of the Vance Monument. (Pack Memorial Library.)

Asheville ended trolley service in 1934, and by the beginning of the war, most of the tracks had been paved over. By order of the Asheville City Council, 1,100 gross tons of metal in the form of trolley rails were sold to the Metals Reserve Company for $1. Here a man pulls up the tracks near Frisbee's Grocery. (Library of Congress.)

Mars Hill College students chipped in to the war effort as well, collecting old keys, two bells, and other scrap. The college saw a one-third drop in enrollment, mostly men, by 1944. The 1944 edition of *The Hilltop*, Mars Hill College's yearbook, complained of a "boy shortage." (Liston B. Ramsey Center for Regional Studies, Mars Hill College Archives.)

Barbara Lashley remembers her Scout troop going "door to door collecting aluminum and scrap iron. We would take it to this big bin at Pack Square. People would give us all kinds of metal like car parts and pots and pans—stuff like that. I also remember going with my troop every Saturday morning to St. Joseph's Hospital where we would roll bandages for Bundles for Britain." (Pack Memorial Library.)

Mrs. Julia Ray of Asheville recalls: "The new troops would leave from the front of Courthouse early in the morning. Our community would be organized to meet them there with donuts and coffee—so they would not leave feeling like they were on their own. Our daughter, Wilma [seen here], was 5 or so and she wanted to do something to make a contribution. She kept talking to us about it and explaining how she wanted to help. We took a basket and filled it with donuts. She would be with us at 6:00 am to pass the food out to the soldiers."

Just as adults contributed to the war effort through buying war bonds (as seen here), dealing with rationing, and supporting the soldiers, so, too, did children. Kids would save war stamps—at 10¢ apiece they were more affordable than war bonds. Schools would compete to see who could collect the most pounds in iron or raise the most money in war stamps. (Pack Memorial Library.)

The Asheville School, a private boarding school, gave students an opportunity to see a movie on Friday nights. The cost of admission was a war bond. This gimmick came about after the *Ashnoca*, the Asheville School's newspaper, complained that students were spending more in the snack bar than on war bonds. (Asheville School Archives.)

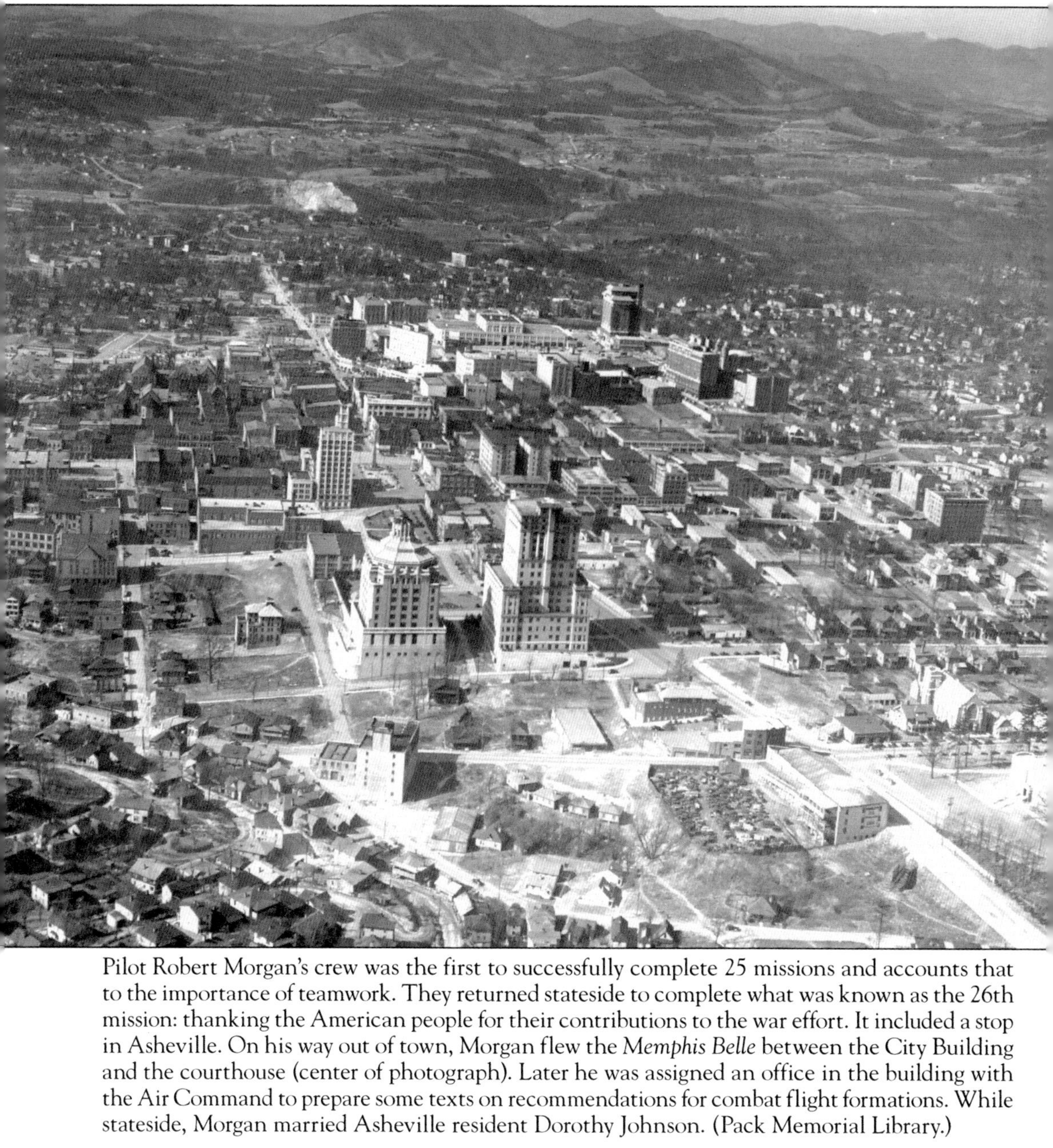

Pilot Robert Morgan's crew was the first to successfully complete 25 missions and accounts that to the importance of teamwork. They returned stateside to complete what was known as the 26th mission: thanking the American people for their contributions to the war effort. It included a stop in Asheville. On his way out of town, Morgan flew the *Memphis Belle* between the City Building and the courthouse (center of photograph). Later he was assigned an office in the building with the Air Command to prepare some texts on recommendations for combat flight formations. While stateside, Morgan married Asheville resident Dorothy Johnson. (Pack Memorial Library.)

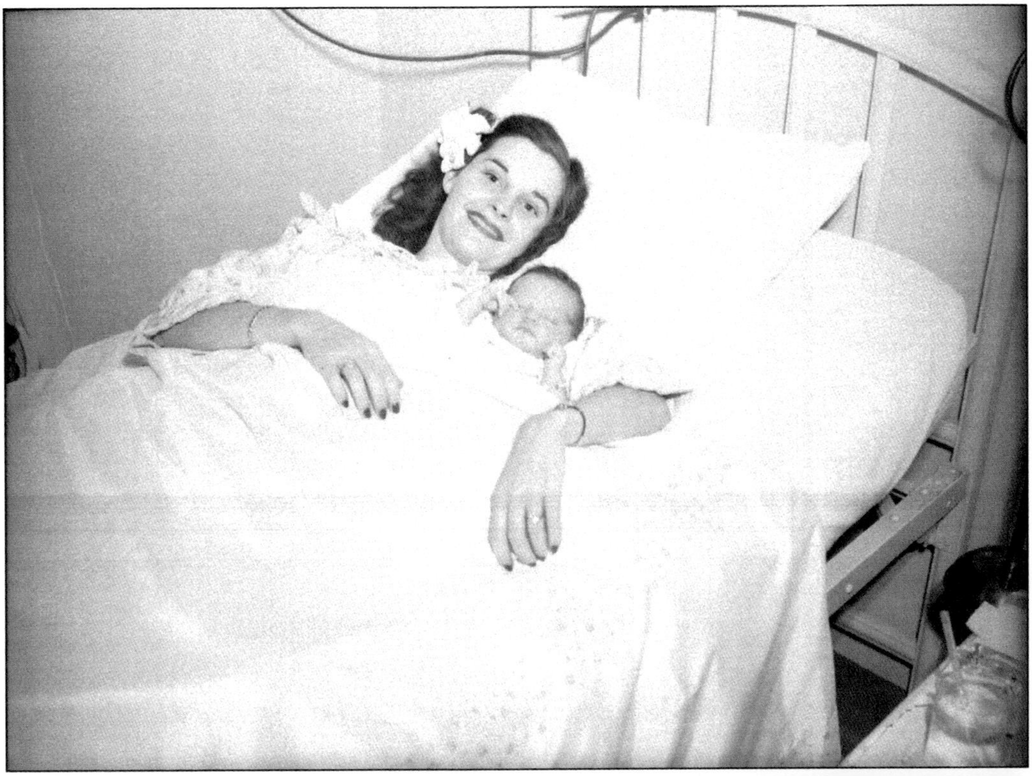

In late 1943, Morgan signed on to fly B-29s in the Pacific theater, where he completed an additional 26 missions. His wife, Dorothy (seen here), the namesake of his B-29, *Dauntless Dotty*, gave birth to their daughter, Sandra, in November 1944 while Morgan was making bombing runs on Japan. (Ball Collection, Ramsey Library, UNCA.)

The war divided families, making for some very traumatic separations. Many families took photographs of service members in front of their homes, documenting time with their kids before shipping overseas. Here Bill Buchanan posed with his oldest child, William, before shipping out with the 9th Infantry Division, First Army.

James "Pop" Hollandsworth, who after the war became a famous figure at the Asheville School, left his five-month-old son Jimmy at home. He sent his son frequent letters, among them one with a drawing of a dog: "Bet you've just about forgotten your Daddy. Bow wow!!! Remember me!" (Asheville School Archives.)

Harold Schaill (left) served in the Pacific with the 77th Anti-aircraft Battalion, which consisted mostly of black soldiers. This photograph, taken on his wedding day, shows him kneeling next to his wife, Mary. He carried this picture in his wallet throughout the war.

In Asheville, USO (United Service Organizations) Clubs operated in a number of locations, providing a place for card playing, dancing, and visiting. Margaret Ensley, 18 at the time, recalls: "The YMCA on Woodfin Street in downtown Asheville had weekly USO dances on Saturday nights. Many soldiers came from surrounding military installations in and around Asheville. Camp Croft in Spartanburg was also within traveling distance." (Ball Collection, Ramsey Library, UNCA.)

The Young Men's Institute (YMI), a center for the African American community since 1892, placed the following announcement in the Asheville *Citizen* on December 4, 1942: "The USO Lounge for Negro servicemen and women, located at the YMI building on Eagle Street, will observe its initial opening this afternoon at 5 o'clock. The Rev. J. M. Cole pastor of St. Mathias Episcopal church will be in charge." (Black Highlander Collection, Ramsey Library, UNCA.)

The Laurentine Canteen, in the basement of St. Lawrence Church, provided a place for dances and entertainment. Lucille Guilka Lamy of Asheville, 16 at the time, remembers: "In Asheville there was no place for the soldiers to go . . . so we decided to open the USO canteen, and my mother herself went out and begged all the furniture—lamps, tables, chairs, everything—to furnish the place." (Pack Memorial Library.)

It was at the Laurentine Canteen that Lucille Guilka met her future husband, Emile Raymond Lamy of Hartford, Connecticut, who was serving in the army at Moore General Hospital. Guilka said she would not marry him until he was discharged from the army because, as she put it, "I don't want that worry. It's enough of a worry not being married to you."

The Jewish Community Center (JCC) on Charlotte Street hosted local soldiers and those from Spartanburg's Camp Croft. Phyllis Sultan of Asheville recalls: "A bunch of people got together where every weekend soldiers were invited—they were bused up. We called around and got homes that would take them—it was no problem. We had committees who organized programs like dances at the Jewish Community Center." (Asheville Jewish Community Center.)

Sultan was one of the key organizers of the JCC USO: "Just as many soldiers as we could house would come up—maybe 20. The host would give them a place to sleep and breakfast. . . . In this picture there are four of us with Camp Croft soldiers." From left to right are Phyllis Sultan, Sylvia Patla, Helen May, and Doris Patla with unidentified Camp Croft soldiers.

If couples wanted to marry quickly, they would head down the mountain to Greenville, South Carolina, where there was no waiting period between license and ceremony. Others held a more traditional service. Morris Fox, in navy uniform, married hometown bride Ruth Schandler at the Jewish Community Center. Later he worked in cryptanalysis in Washington, D.C., to break the Japanese code.

Raised a Quaker, Greensboro's Charles Hendricks knew that as a pacifist he could not fight. While his brothers went into noncombatant service as medics, Hendricks became a conscientious objector (CO). He spent the war near Marion at the Buck Creek Service Camp, which was operated and funded by the Quaker community. While there, Hendricks helped build Crabtree Park on the Blue Ridge Parkway and fought forest fires in that area.

Hendricks said that for the most part people tolerated his position, but the mood of the country at war made being a CO an unpopular choice. "But I knew for me it was the right thing to do. One time I went into Marion to buy a bathing suit. When the salesperson asked me where I was stationed I told him I was at Buck Creek. He said 'I don't have anything to sell you.' I was sympathetic to issues raised by the war and to the need for solving problems, but not by killing people. The government set up these CO camps where I felt like I could serve my country but not kill people. Some of my friends wouldn't even do that and would rather go to prison—which they did." (Top and bottom, James Fox, Swarthmore Peace College.)

With the men off fighting, the burden of tending the farms fell to those left behind. Women and children provided a great deal of the farming labor. In the top photograph from 1943, 13-year-old Rose Cook of Leicester takes her turn at the plow. The Farmers Federation, a cooperative designed to improve the lives of WNC farmers, helped increase agricultural productivity by introducing new breeds of animals and improved farming methods. In 1944 the Farmers Federation opened a meat locker plant on Broadway in downtown Asheville. Overflow hams and pork shoulders hang in the Asheville meat locker in the lower image from 1945. (Top and bottom, James G. K. McClure Collection, Appalachian Archives, Mars Hill College.)

Big Witch Creek's Lavinia Chiltoskie, a Cherokee Central School student, demonstrated home canning methods for the *Farmers Federation News* in 1944. According to the article which accompanied this photograph, "4 Day Schools and Central School at Cherokee canned 24,560 quarts and dehydrated 5,680 quarts of food last year." Chiltoskie's teacher, Gertrude Flanagan estimated that Cherokee families canned an additional 100,000 quarts. (James G. K. McClure Collection, Appalachian Archives, Mars Hill College.)

The secret facility at Oak Ridge, Tennessee, needed electricity to produce the uranium-235 used in the atomic bomb that destroyed Hiroshima. Fontana Dam would provide it. Jobs were advertised throughout the nation. As was the law of the land, Fontana Village was segregated. The school for black students is pictured here. (TVA Collection, National Archives.)

During the war, many American businesses retooled their factories for war production. Such was the case at Asheville's Dave Steel. They made parts for the landing ships, LST-325s, that were used for beach landings in Normandy, Italy, Tripoli, and the Philippines (bottom). A dam employee remembered, "We had trucks running all the time. As soon as we completed one [section] the truck was on the road" to take it to Charleston, South Carolina, where the ship was assembled. (Top, Dave Steel; Bottom, Library of Congress.)

In 1944, Dave Steel was awarded the "E" (for excellence) Award, which was observed with ceremonies in Charleston and Asheville. At the award ceremony, the company held a dance for the employees. The company service flag is visible to the right. (Courtesy of Dave Steel.)

Periodically the federal government brought promotional tours through the region to maintain support for the war. This photograph, taken at the Dave Steel site on the corner of Depot Street and Clingman Avenue, documents such a tour. (Courtesy of Dave Steel.)

Some 930 employees of Black Mountain's Beacon Manufacturing, nearly half the workforce, joined the military. Women were already an important part of the Beacon team, but they became

even more critical during the war. This picture was taken at a Christmas dinner during the war. (Swannanoa Valley Museum.)

Beacon Manufacturing made woolen blankets for the armed forces during the war. Once geared up, they became the third largest producer of these blankets in the United States. By war's end, they had delivered over seven million blankets. (Swannanoa Valley Museum.)

Beacon employees pose here with employees of Southern Railroad and a train engine. During the war, sabotage at industrial sites was a major problem. To prevent losses at Beacon, the federal government put a U.S. Army colonel in charge of security. (Swannanoa Valley Museum.)

On February 8, 1945, a disagreement between the union workers (right) and the American Enka Corporation (bottom) led to a strike. The company was unwilling to offer workers paid lunches or to pay higher wages for less desirable shifts, such as night shifts. Enka manufactured rayon for tires, which the military critically needed as the troops rapidly advanced through Europe. Lt. Col. Paul Hines, chief of the labor branch of the U.S. Army Command, appealed to workers to return to work: "Every hour of the production of the rayon cord used in tires that is lost at Enka means a loss of about 150 to 200 tires that are badly needed just now. . . . On one highway in France we are chewing up 5000 tires a day." Eleven days later, Roosevelt ordered the War Department to take over plant management. (Top and bottom, Ball Collection, Ramsey Library, UNCA.)

At the Champion Paper Mill in Canton, women like Ruth Scruggs, seen in the upper photograph operating a 72-inch boring mill in 1943, did a great deal of the work. They also volunteered for the troops. The lower photograph, also from 1943, shows Canton women volunteering to fold surgical dressings for the Red Cross. (Top and bottom, Canton Area Historical Museum.)

This photograph, from a 1943 edition of Champion's newsletter, *The Log*, shows a truck rigged up to deal with the strictures of the ration board. The wooden wheels bypassed the tire ration, while "gas produced by burning charcoal in a metal gas-producer attached to the side of the truck" eased Champion's gasoline rations. (Canton Area Historical Museum.)

Sayles Bleachery also gained federal contracts, in this case to finish khakis and material for parachutes. The material arrived gray and would be bleached white. These contracts kept the company and its employees quite busy, especially considering that 165 men and 1 woman left Sayles to enter the military. (Ball Collection, Ramsey Library, UNCA.)

The United States spent approximately $2 billion in North Carolina for the purchase of manufactured goods during the war. Black Mountain Hosiery's owner, Benjamin Hunter, managed to obtain with the help of Sen. Robert Reynolds a federal contract to provide socks for the military. By

war's end, the plant produced 60 percent of the production of socks for the army and navy. (Swannanoa Valley Museum.)

Much of the organized entertainment was geared toward single men and women. Married women had fewer options. As Asheville's Mary Ellen Wolcott (left, with husband, Bill) put it, there wasn't much to do "if you didn't have a man to take you out." Many spent time writing letters to their husbands. Wolcott and several other women formed the APO (Army Post Office) Wives Club. According to Mrs. Wolcott, the club's main objective was to offer an outlet to women "strained by war." It also served as an opportunity for women married to servicemen to, in the words of APO Wives Club cofounder Mary Schaill, "mostly talk and gossip." In the lower photograph is a meeting of the APO Wives Club. At first row center is visiting speaker Filipino general Valdez, with Mary Ellen Wolcott to the left and Mary Schaill to the right.

The Langren Hotel, since demolished, sat at the corner of Broadway and College Street. It hosted community meetings throughout the war. The APO Wives Club's 30–35 members met here monthly for lunch. The Next of Kin Club, which grew from 14 members at their first meeting to 208 at their final meeting, met at the hotel every month in the afternoon. (Ball Collection, Ramsey Library, UNCA.)

BUY BONDS FOR PRISONERS OF WAR—Mrs. Clyde W. Bradley, center, and Mrs. G. L. Leslie, Sr., right, are shown buying war bonds at Ivey's bond booth for their two sons who are prisoners of war in Germany. Mrs. Bradley, whose son, Lt. William Bradley, is a prisoner, bought $1,500 worth of bonds for him, and Mrs. Leslie bought $1,000 worth of bonds for Lt. G. L. Leslie, Jr., who is in the same prison camp. Mrs. Bradley qualified for captain in the Blue Star brigade of the women's division in the Sixth War Loan drive, with sales to 20 individuals. Other promotions announced were: Mrs. J. Frank Crowell, nurses' association, sales to 20 individuals, captain; Mrs. H. Bomberger, Elks' auxiliary, sales to 30 individuals, major, and Mrs. Harvey Holleman, Fortnightly club, sales to 50 individuals, colonel. The Next of Kin club, of which Mrs. Bradley is president and Mrs. Leslie is vice-president, was credited with $2,875 in bond sales in two and one half hours while the club had charge of the booth. Miss Florence Stevens, is shown at the left, selling the bonds.

As the war dragged on and more servicemen were taken prisoner, families at home needed support. On September 8, 1944, the Next of Kin Club assembled for an organizational meeting at the Langren Hotel in downtown Asheville. Typically if a POW were nominated for an award, the military would present the award to a parent. The Next of Kin Club often hosted these ceremonies. Much of their budget was spent on sending flowers to the families of servicemen missing in action. Mrs. J. L. Hall, secretary, kept a detailed scrapbook containing not only the organization's very formal minutes, but also hundreds of articles relating to POWs, many of them heart-wrenching stories. President Bradley and Vice President Leslie buy war bonds (top). The lower image shows two telegrams Mrs. Hall received regarding her son.

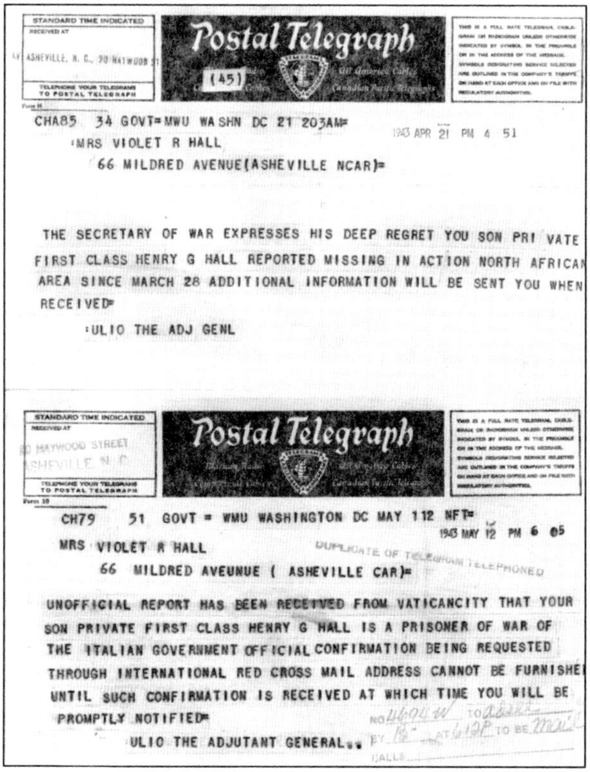

Postal Telegraph

CHA85 34 GOVT=WMU WASHN DC 21 203AM=
1943 APR 21 PM 4 51
MRS VIOLET R HALL
66 MILDRED AVENUE(ASHEVILLE NCAR)=

THE SECRETARY OF WAR EXPRESSES HIS DEEP REGRET YOU SON PRIVATE FIRST CLASS HENRY G HALL REPORTED MISSING IN ACTION NORTH AFRICAN AREA SINCE MARCH 28 ADDITIONAL INFORMATION WILL BE SENT YOU WHEN RECEIVED=
ULIO THE ADJ GENL

Postal Telegraph

CH79 51 GOVT = WMU WASHINGTON DC MAY 112 NFT=
1943 MAY 12 PM 6 05
MRS VIOLET R HALL
66 MILDRED AVEUNUE (ASHEVILLE CAR)=

UNOFFICIAL REPORT HAS BEEN RECEIVED FROM VATICANCITY THAT YOUR SON PRIVATE FIRST CLASS HENRY G HALL IS A PRISONER OF WAR OF THE ITALIAN GOVERNMENT OFFICIAL CONFIRMATION BEING REQUESTED THROUGH INTERNATIONAL RED CROSS MAIL ADDRESS CANNOT BE FURNISHED UNTIL SUCH CONFIRMATION IS RECEIVED AT WHICH TIME YOU WILL BE PROMPTLY NOTIFIED=
ULIO THE ADJUTANT GENERAL.

Students at Western Carolina Teachers College (later Western Carolina University) rushed to join the military. In the top photograph, Pres. H. T. Hunter congratulates 1942 graduating senior Joe Hedden of Sylva, who had already enlisted in the navy. The student body gradually lost most of their male students, as suggested by the lower photograph. The 1945 yearbook announced in its introduction "We are the war generation. . . . not one man is graduating." The junior class only had two male members that year. (Top and bottom, Hunter Library, Western Carolina University.)

Black Mountain College, like many small colleges around the country, saw a dwindling number of men (and to a lesser degree, women) among their ranks. By 1943, only one male student remained on campus. The faculty suffered likewise, losing most of its young male members. (North Carolina State Archives.)

The Asheville Farm School, later Warren Wilson College, was already under financial duress in 1940 because of decreased funding by the Presbyterian Church. It became a junior college to help deal with this loss of funding. With the prospect of war looming, the school decided to accept women in 1942. In 1943, the college accepted two Japanese young women—Kuni Ohama (left) and Sally Yasusaga—who had previously been interned in camps in the western part of the country. (Warren Wilson College Archives.)

In August 1943, another Japanese student, Kuniko Hirokawa, seen here standing third from left, came to campus. The FBI cleared the Japanese students as "good American citizens" before they came to the school. (Warren Wilson College Archives.)

Warren Wilson's homemaking classes helped in the conservation of needed war materials by recycling clothes. An October 1942 edition of the Wilson *Echo*, the school newspaper, reported that students had made skirts from old knickers. (Warren Wilson College Archives.)

As the war effort siphoned off laborers, the Asheville School had to appeal to some of its students to carry out much of the work on campus. According to the 1942 annual, "This year, in contributing to the national war effort by adopting a program of self-help, the boys are taking care of their rooms, making their beds and some are waiting on tables." These boys were among the first students to serve meals on campus. (Asheville School Archives.)

With the implementation of rationing, many items such as sugar, Jell-o, and canned goods were in short supply. Folks were encouraged to grow victory gardens. The Asheville School did just that in 1943, growing their own potatoes, and later other vegetables, under the direction of Thomas Bell. (Asheville School Archives.)

According to a 1943 issue of the *Ashnoca*, the Asheville School's newspaper, "Of the 17 boys of last year's graduating class who have reported to the Alumni office, almost all are in either the armed forces or in some specialized military training program." The school obtained its own service flag, indicating the number of service members the school provided. By 1945, some 551 alumni had entered military service. (Asheville School Archives.)

The Asheville School sought to prepare their students for the war effort. All students were required to attend calisthenics four times a week. To help students obtain skills vital to the nation, community members came in to work with students. This picture shows students in the radio club, who received support from WWNC, a local radio station. (Asheville School Archives.)

Buncombe County was a regional center for wounded soldiers. The Veterans Administration medical center at the time was more generally known as Oteen Hospital. Members of the Next of Kin Club gave gifts to patients here to ease their recovery. (Pack Memorial Library.)

During the First World War, the government made use of the Kenilworth Inn as a hospital. In the Second World War, the navy acquired it for use as the Naval Convalescent Hospital. (Ball Collection, Ramsey Library, UNCA.)

In 1943, the army took over Norburn Hospital, seen here in its Montford neighborhood location. After the war, the Champion Paper Mill donated money in honor of the "Champion family" lost in the war to help expand Norburn, which moved to Biltmore Avenue and was renamed Memorial Mission Hospital. (Pack Memorial Library.)

Farther down the road, the Lake Lure Inn became a rehabilitation center, known as the Army Air Force Redistribution Rest Camp, for veterans who were wounded in spirit. At the time, descriptors such as "combat fatigue" and "nerve strain" were euphemisms that now go under the heading post-traumatic stress disorder. (North Carolina State Archives.)

Women's Army Corps nurses arrive at Moore General Hospital, built in 1942 on the grounds of Oteen's State Test Farm. Nearly 5,000 workers helped speed its construction. The 1,520-bed hospital mainly treated patients with respiratory problems but also handled burn victims. Assigned to work on the facility were 250 German POWs. (Ball Collection, Ramsey Library, UNCA.)

The Gray Ladies, so named because of their gray uniforms, of the American Red Cross assisted wounded soldiers by offering various non-medical assistance, such as writing letters, reading, or showing them around the area. The wounded soldiers coming through Moore General Hospital kept area Gray Ladies (seen here) busy. (Swannanoa Valley Museum.)

Margaret Rose Ensley (left) often sang at Moore General Hospital, recalling: "The wounded were brought in a special hospital train. . . . A party was planned for their arrival and USO girls were called. You always wore your prettiest long dress and a smile on your face. Sometimes it was hard to smile when you saw their wounds and agony. At the dances you talked to them and danced with them if they felt up to it."

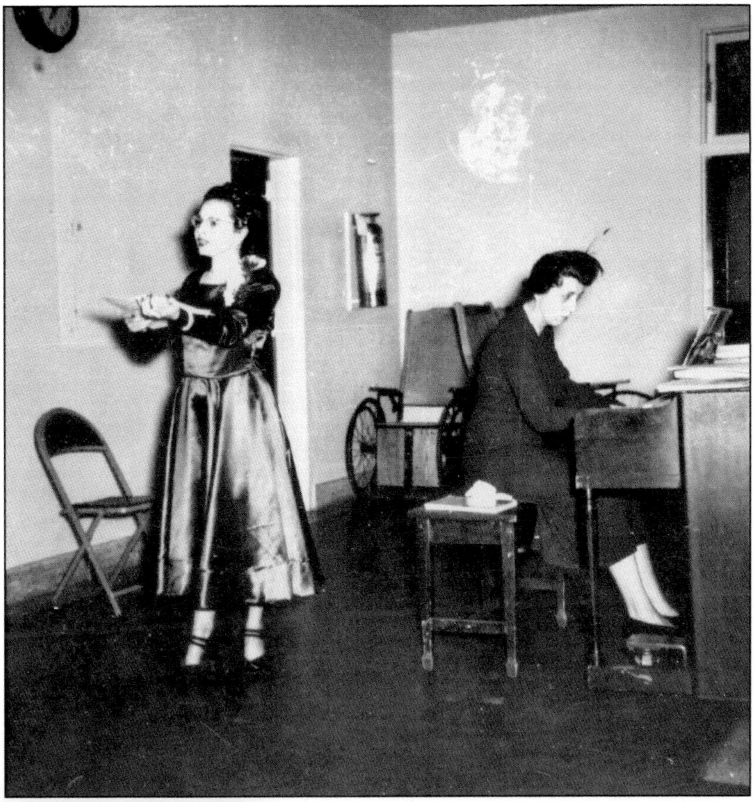

Many women volunteered to help entertain the troops as well as relieve the nurses for other work. Local resident Phyllis Sultan recalled volunteering at Moore General Hospital with the Red Cross.

In March 1945, Eleanor Roosevelt, who traveled the United States throughout the war, visited Asheville, addressing a meeting of the Council of Southern Mountain Workers at Montreat, visiting Black Mountain College, and speaking to patients at Moore General Hospital. (Swannanoa Valley Museum.)

A McDowell County business created this window display to showcase the Women's Army Corps (WAC) Enrollment Campaign. (North Carolina State Archives.)

The American Red Cross needed substantial funding to provide its relief services. Louis Lipinsky (seen here)—Asheville businessman, philanthropist, and namesake of the main UNCA auditorium—chaired Buncombe County's Red Cross War Fund Drive from 1942 to 1945. The entire community stepped in to help: Ivey's department store and Carolina Power and Light sponsored full-page advertisements in the local newspapers. (Lipinsky Collection, Ramsey Library, UNCA.)

Even area schools contributed to the Red Cross. By April 1, 1943, pupils of David Miller Junior High School had contributed $360. Allen Home and Black Mountain Negro School were the first area schools to achieve 100 percent enrollment in the Junior Red Cross. Some of this money funded Asheville's four Red Cross Production Rooms, one of which was located at David Miller Junior High, above. (Ball Collection, Ramsey Library, UNCA.)

Mrs. Hugh Lamb (top, on right), the Buncombe County Red Cross's chief cloth cutter during the war years, ran a production room in the old Haywood Road post office (bottom, second from left). She was once described in the Asheville *Citizen* as having "a genuine talent for handling a pattern, a bolt of cloth and a pair of scissors." (Bottom, Ball Collection, Ramsey Library, UNCA.)

Emily Meares (right), daughter of Mrs. J. E. Meares of Kimberly Avenue, became the program director of an American Red Cross Club in Southport, England. The club served as a hostel and entertainment center for soldiers. She at times lent money to soldiers. Occasionally unwed pregnant British women would ask her to track down servicemen who had fathered the child. (Emily Meares Collection, Buncombe County Chapter of the American Red Cross.)

Red Cross Clubs also sponsored sporting events for service members overseas. Soldier Sanders of Cherokee played on a Red Cross basketball team while stationed in Great Britain. His team went on to win the Northern Ireland Air Corps Championship in 1943. They, however, lost the 1943 ETO (European Theater of Operations) Tournament in the quarterfinals. At some point, Sanders (standing second from right) drew glasses on himself.

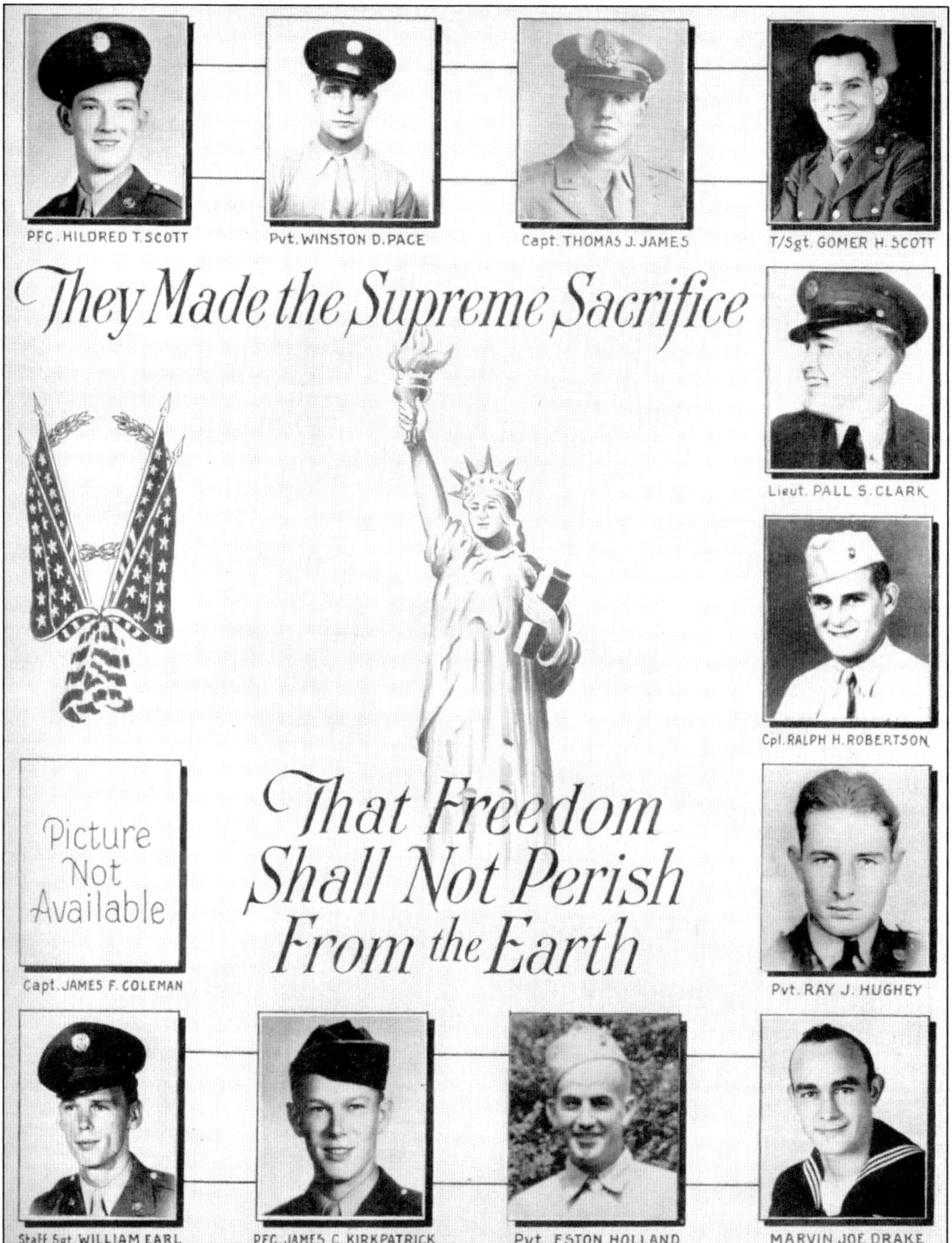

Champion Paper Company put in its company newsletter, *The Log*, this memorial to employees who gave their lives in the war. Through the war years, *The Log* reminded workers to consider the service members. (Canton Area Historical Museum.)

Three

FRONTLINES

The war undeniably transformed the face of WNC and all of America. The changes happening on the frontlines were even more perilous and personal. The brutal cost of fighting fascism meant more and even younger service members went into action. Men serving under Landon Roberts referred to him as "Pappy" because of his advanced age of 22. George Hilbert, of Black Mountain, remembers being trained when he was only 18: "They had me handling dynamite. I couldn't have a bb gun or a bike as a kid." These young people had to grow up fast; they were entrusted with great responsibilities. And yet the tug of duty was great. Clifford Longcoy of Black Mountain, who joined up at age 17, remembers: "I saw the flag waving. . . . When I enlisted, you had to weigh 120 pounds, so I ate bananas all the way to Raleigh."

Karl Straus, who worked for his Uncle Harry Straus at Brevard's Ecusta plant, was also eager to volunteer, but his "Enemy Alien" status prevented him from doing so—even though he was a Jewish refugee from Germany. Later he was allowed to enlist: "My unit was going to Japan, while I wanted to go to Germany."

Nurse Bertha Moore found that many soldiers would leave her field hospital in North Africa before being released, essentially going AWOL, in order to rejoin their units at the front. As she put it, "It sounds like they were stark raving mad" for wanting to go back to the fighting. However, the men felt such camaraderie with their fellow soldiers that they did not want to let them down. This selflessness deeply impressed Moore.

The great menace facing service members, the nation, and indeed the world, forced the United States to examine itself, individually and collectively, to assess its mettle. It is here the nation found the trust in each other, the optimism, and the hope necessary to move forward, despite the risks.

PFC Fain Brooks left his home in the Newfound community in Leicester, North Carolina, to face the unknown enemy overseas. This emblematic photograph graced the cover of the 1943 *Forgotten Pioneer,* a pamphlet distributed by the Farmers Federation. (James G. K. McClure Collection, Appalachian Archives, Mars Hill College.)

At the onset of the war, several thousand troops worked to secure the Philippine peninsula of Bataan. Here U.S. engineers, including Sylva's Walter Middleton, began building airports. Robbinsville native Wayne Carringer, at the time a staff sergeant with the 27th Bomb Group in the Army Air Corps, was stationed on Bataan and remembers that all their supplies, including their aircraft, were diverted to Australia. As Japanese forces made an aggressive assault in the Pacific, U.S. forces on Bataan were trapped without support and living on half rations. Middleton's company was one of the last to leave the front lines. After their surrender, U.S. and Philippine troops endured what has come to be known as the Bataan Death March (top photo). Walter Middleton (in lower picture, at right) and another ex-POW celebrated their birthdays at Moore General Hospital during their first year back in the United States. (Library of Congress.)

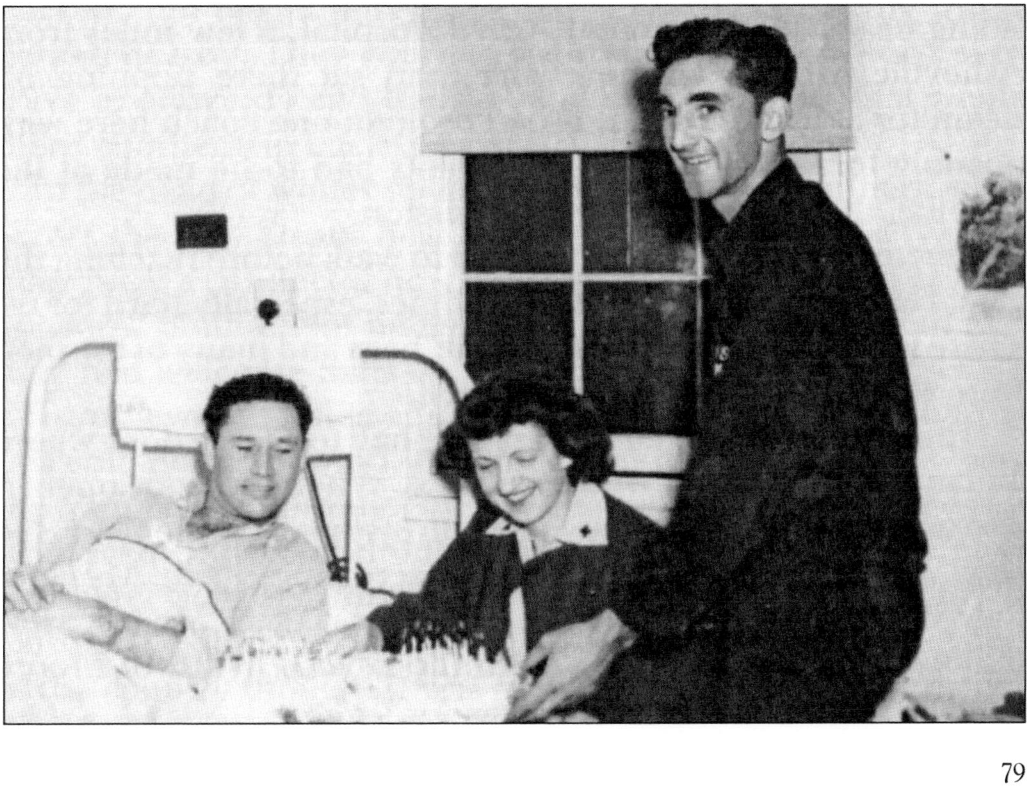

By 1942, Robert Morgan (fifth from left) with his B-17, the *Memphis Belle*, took part in the earliest U.S. bombings over Europe against the practiced German Luftwaffe. The attrition rate of aircrews at that early point in the war reached a staggering 80 percent. As Morgan put it, "We'd sit down to breakfast in the morning with ten and come back with two." Morale sagged as flight crews lost their friends. The military brass realized that it had to offer crews a goal. Morgan said, "The generals came up with this idea that [if] you finish 25 missions you could go home. That gave us something to shoot at."

Jesse Ledbetter grew up on a dairy farm in Arden. A month before the Japanese bombed Pearl Harbor, Ledbetter's father died and Jesse, at the tender age of 19, became responsible for the family farm. But his heart was set on the military. He already held a private pilot's license, and by 20, he was both married and a pilot in the Army Air Corps.

Robert Bolinder flew a P-61 Black Widow. On the first night of the Battle of the Bulge, he took off at midnight. When he returned to his base, he found out that he was to fly another mission that night due to "a lot of activity." He took off again at 3 a.m. "That was the most violent hour of flight that I flew. . . . the sky was full of targets."

Alan Neilson (top, on left), with his pilot "Pappy" in England. Neilson served with the 8th Air Force from September 1943 until November 1945. His experiences differed greatly from those of Robert Morgan. By the time he began bombing German forces, the skies were crowded with U.S. planes. The attrition rate had also turned around; consequently crews were expected to fly more missions. Pilots and crews faced great danger from flak, seen in the photograph below, courtesy of Neilson.

Planes were often named after something dear to the pilot or crew. This B-17 Flying Fortress bears the name "Rutherford County, NC." (North Carolina State Archives.)

The Tuskegee Airmen were the first African American pilots to serve in the Army Air Corps. Initially they flew air patrol. Later they escorted bombers into Germany, holding the unprecedented record of escorting 200 missions without a loss. George B. Greenlee Jr., brother of local resident Julia Ray, graduated from the Tuskegee Institute as a pilot in the 332nd Fighter Squadron. (Library of Congress.)

Both Henry E. Colton Jr. (top, with nephew John O. Colton Jr. and sister-in-law, Josephine) and his brother John (below) were pilots flying missions out of Britain in May 1944 when Henry went to John's base for a weekend together. Henry remembered: "When I got to his base, I told the Duty Officer that I was Ensign Colton, and I wanted to see my brother Lt. Colton. He told me to wait and went into the guardhouse. After a few minutes, he returned and said: 'Mr. Colton, I regret to tell you that your brother was flying a mission May 22 over Kiel Canal in Germany. He was shot down and killed. He is dead.'" Henry wrote a letter breaking the news to John's widow.

Over 200 of WNC's troops suffered as prisoners of war. Most of the prisoners during the war were members of the Army Air Corps, who spent a great deal of time flying over enemy territory. Statistically the numbers were against the flight crews. Here the 8th Air Force flies over Marienburg, Germany. (Library of Congress.)

Several graduates of Lee Edwards High School had a most remarkable class reunion in, of all places, Stalag Luft 3, a German POW camp. Bill Bradley, Joe Davis, and G. L. Leslie (pictured here) were "all good friends" back in high school. In camp, they kept each other going. Conditions in the camp were often quite poor, though according to Leslie, "we had more food than the average German."

While bombing over Germany, Soldier Sanders (left) of Cherokee, a member of the Western Band of the Cherokee Nation, was shot down over Magdeburg, Germany. He and the other nine crewmembers on his B-17 safely landed, though angry German farmers immediately killed the radio operator. Soldier and the remaining crewmen were rounded up and eventually sent to Stalag Luft 2. His wife, Kay, of the Eastern Band, (lower portrait), recalls receiving a letter a month later that he was missing in action. Later she got a letter stating that her husband was a POW. A month after that, she received a short letter from Soldier through the Red Cross. He explained that he escaped while being transferred to another camp and met up with an advanced team of Patton's Army.

Roland Sargent (right), a B-17 pilot, was shot down, managing to land in the field of some sympathetic Belgian farmers. They contacted the Belgium underground, which helped him and 10 other fliers onto a train. In Paris, the Gestapo stopped and questioned him. They put him in prison and, since he had no military identification, told him, "You'll be treated as a spy and probably shot." Later, due to information the Red Cross provided to the Luftwaffe, he was able to clear up his identity. This photograph was taken shortly after Sargent reached the Belgium underground, which provided the civilian clothes.

Joe Katen was in the China-Burma-India theater where he carried much-needed supplies of gasoline "over the hump" on more than 150 missions. He received five air medals, two Purple Hearts, and two Flying Cross medals before returning stateside in November 1945.

Dick Harshaw was inducted into the army in June 1943. He trained at Camp Croft, South Carolina, to be a light truck driver. He arrived in November 1944 in Europe, where he served in Ardennes, Rhineland, and Central Europe, being promoted during that time to private, first class.

Kyle Morgan (top photograph) of Asheville, a 1940 graduate of Lee Edwards High School, joined the Army Air Corps in 1943. He served most of his time in England as a radio repairman, an assignment based in part on his work experience at Freck's Radio and Supply Company on Biltmore Avenue, seen in the lower photograph on the right (beside Sterchi's). (Pack Memorial Library.)

Asheville native Leo Finkelstein (above, left) was inducted into the Army Air Corps in 1943 at age 38. He served as a clerk, chiefly in the Philippines. While in the Pacific, he regularly sent letters to the Lions Club of Asheville, of which he was a past president. He left his business, Finklestein's Pawn Shop (seen in the lower photograph), to serve overseas. After the war, he resumed running the shop. (Top and bottom, Ball Collection, Ramsey Library, UNCA.)

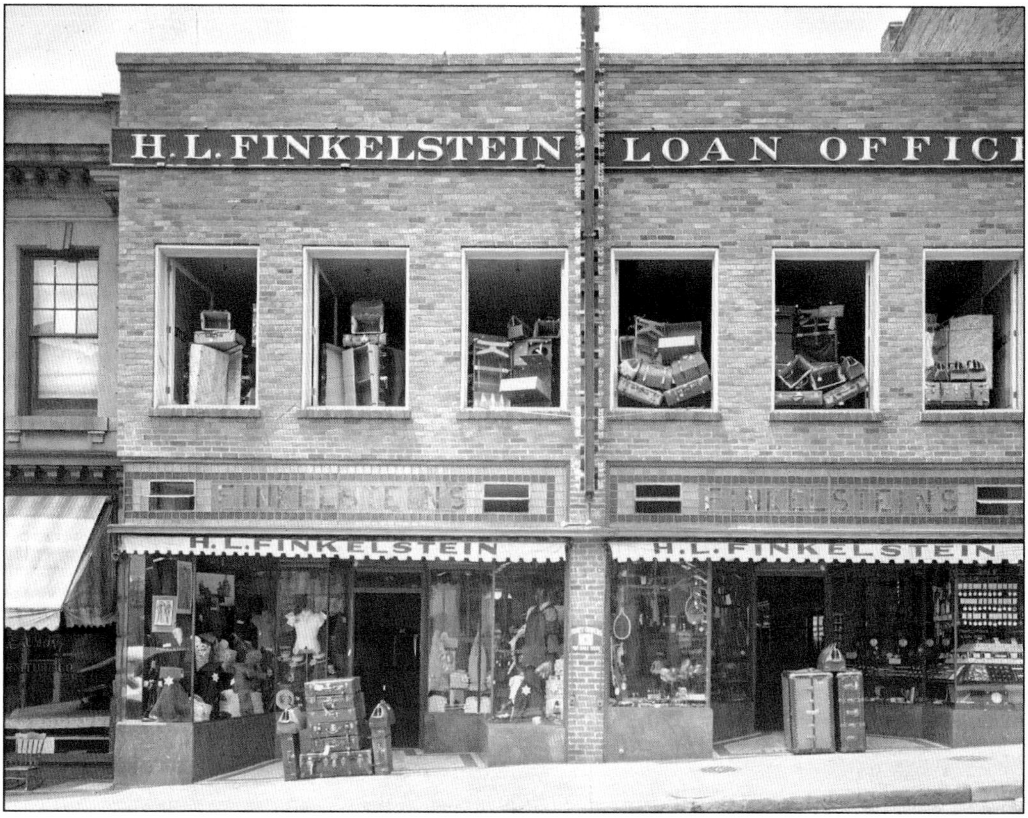

During the war, Marie Colton translated and decoded Spanish language documents the government intercepted. One day, her code no longer seemed to work, so she alerted her superiors. "The next day a picture appeared on my desk. You could see this man's hairy hands holding what was the new code." She clearly recalled that his watch read 3 a.m. Responding to her report, someone had "acquired" the new code and delivered it to her. This window into the world of espionage gave her rather mundane desk job new excitement.

John Rosenthal (left) was a refugee before the war and spoke excellent German. He was assigned to the German Intelligence Unit with the army, where initially he translated newspapers to gauge the mood of the people. He remembered a German attack on a theater: "It knocked off the front of the theatre where the screen was, killing all the people. Soldiers and dates in the balcony were all still there—covered with white dust—like wax figures. They were all dead." Almost 500 people, many of them Allied soldiers, were killed in that attack. Rosenthal passed through Asheville on the train on his way to Camp Croft, South Carolina, (lower photograph) in 1943. Its beauty struck him. It took him almost 40 years, and retirement from his job at the Library of Congress, to return.

Asheville's Henry Baker joined the Alamo Scouts, a forerunner of the Special Forces. In one mission, Baker's unit built an airstrip so a plane could land behind enemy lines. "We set up signals and were able to evacuate [Philippine General Carlos Romulo's] son, wife and brother. There was no room for me. I had to walk out. It took six or seven days and I traveled at night."

Edward W. Pearson Jr. (seen here with his mother, Annis E. Bradshaw Pearson, at left and his sister, Annette Pearson Cotton, right) joined the army in 1943. The Stephens-Lee High School graduate went on to become Asheville's first black disc jockey, working for WLOS, as well as a self-employed photographer. (Pack Memorial Library.)

Black Mountain's Ernest "Andy" Andrews (top) clearly remembered the convoy that brought him to France as part of the D-Day invasion (bottom photograph). He was to be part of the third wave, landing on the beach around sunset. They were not able to make this goal due to the number of dead on the beach. The deck officer at the time commented, "You're not going in until enough guys are killed." He remembered the fear, the adrenaline, the unknown: "Courage doesn't replace fear, but it's the mastery of fear," he commented. Though they ended up landing in the early morning, their machine guns—"too heavy to land with"—didn't arrive on the beach until midday. They picked up guns from among the dead. Andrews distinctly remembers thinking, "What in the world am I doing here?" (Bottom, Library of Congress.)

December 1944 found Reuben Taylor, a member of the Eastern Band of the Cherokee Nation, at the front in Holland. He and his peers would select bombed-out craters to serve as their foxholes, "an old Indian trick." During this time, while returning from patrol, he was shot in the knee by a sniper. Within days, he was back at the front, where the Battle of the Bulge roared.

The 30th Infantry Division as a National Guard unit initially drew its ranks from North Carolina, South Carolina, Georgia, and Tennessee. After being federalized in 1940, it began drawing soldiers from a wider national audience. Known to other Allied forces as "the workhorse of the Western Front" and to the Nazis as "Roosevelt's SS," the 30th opened the way for Patton's troops to advance through France and into Germany. (North Carolina State Archives.)

Occasionally entire families sometimes enlisted. Brothers Guy, James, Bill, and Otis Lonon (top, from left to right) grew up in the North Cove section of McDowell County where their family owned a general store. All four brothers returned safely to the United States from overseas service. Likewise Ervin Ray (left) was one of three brothers to join the army, earning their family a three-star service flag. Sometimes families lost multiple children to the war, as in the case of Mr. and Mrs. W. W. Ballew of 4 Hickory Terrace in Asheville, who lost their sons James Robert and Charles William, both firemen in the navy. (Bottom, Augusto Brisco Ray Collection, Mars Hill College Archives.)

Asheville native O. E. Starnes Jr. (right) was a light machine gunner in the 103rd Infantry. As he made his way across Europe on foot, he had no contact with German civilians "except when we ran out of food." This was a frequent problem, as they often outran their supplies. They would "pick up a few leaves of cabbage" or, more rarely, loaves of brown bread. His uncle Hugh Lamb, who owned the RC Cola bottling plant in Asheville (below), mailed Starnes two bottles of RC. After draining one, Starnes was halfway through the other when his buddies noticed what he had. He found it best to share the remainder rather than risk the wrath of his thirsty friends. Sixty years later, he still recalled that moment: "Man, that was a good drink!" (Bottom, Pack Memorial Library.)

Charlie Bonnett (on the left) from Hendersonville dropped out of high school to enlist in the military. He ended up working on security for the Manhattan Project, where research on atomic weapons was conducted. After the war, he finished up his high school diploma, building a reputation as the "old man on campus." His later career was with the Hendersonville Police Department.

George Gash of Hendersonville was an army engineer: "Our motto was first ones in; last ones out. I trained to operate a bulldozer. We crossed over at La Havre, France soon after D-Day. Our job was keeping up with the Army. . . . The shooting was going on all around us. The guy behind you—at your side—he held your life in his hands. And his in yours."

Asheville's Sid Schochet, here with then fiancée Mary, was drafted at 22. Sid's experience in his family's store on Patton Avenue, the Star, helped him become a quartermaster stationed in Columbus, Ohio. Sid recalls: "You could sort of tell when a big operation, such as D-Day, was about to happen. Certain supplies would be ordered well in advance. The supplies would go out as quickly as we got them in."

Charles McAdams of Asheville was 18 when he joined the army. He had been an employee of Biltmore Hardware and was familiar with ordering, stocking, and selling of goods, so he expected to be a quartermaster. Instead he drove supplies to the front line as part of the Red Ball Express. He recalls little sleep or food and the constant danger of being shot at.

World War II also saw the entrance of women into the Marine Corps. Virginia Zimmerman (first row, left, later Virginia Smathers of Arden) entered the USMC in 1943 and became a film projectionist at Camp Lejeune. She and a group of women operated the movie cameras that entertained the men stationed at Lejeune.

In 1942, the Marine Corps built a third training facility at Camp Lejeune in Eastern North Carolina. At the southern end, known as Montford Point, they provided the first training facility for black Marines. Robert Youngdeer, who later was chief of the Eastern Band of the Cherokee Nation, was among the first officers to work with some of the over 20,000 new recruits. (Library of Congress.)

The first USS *Asheville*, pictured here, was a patrol gunboat known as PG-21. The Japanese attacked and destroyed it on March 3, 1942, leaving only one survivor, Fred Brown, who later died in a POW camp in Japan. A patrol frigate (PF-1) replaced PG-21 in December 1942. This ship became the namesake of an entire class of ships—the Asheville Class. (Walter Ashe Collection, Ramsey Library, UNCA.)

Emily Wodniak (left, later Emily Rogers of Black Mountain) enlisted at the age of 29. She was assigned to Pearl Harbor as a ward supervisor. She recalls her work as "easy. We had hospital corpsman who did all the work," though she worked long shifts. She remembers the time as "the best years of my life . . . lots of men, lots of officers, and we had quite a few dances. I loved to dance."

Walter Ashe, descendant of Gov. Samuel and Mary Ashe, was stationed aboard the USS *Asheville* in the 1930s, and in 1941, he transferred to the new battleship *North Carolina*. The *North Carolina* was faster, more heavily armed, and armored than previous battleships. She represented what Ashe called the "new navy." He recalled that the *North Carolina* was "a real morale boost" for the navy in the Pacific. In August 1942, the *North Carolina* was the only battleship to take part in the Guadalcanal invasion when they were torpedoed by a Japanese submarine. The *North Carolina* was able to radio ahead to Pearl Harbor to have the necessary parts fabricated for installation when the ship arrived. Consequently she was only in the repair yard for about two weeks. The lower picture shows a burial at sea. (Top and bottom, North Carolina State Archives.)

Landon Roberts of Marshall led the capture of Minuti Island from the Japanese. They were honored by 6,000 people who "stood in two long rows, like Jesus in Jerusalem, and laid palm fronds across the sand. . . . The women only wore grass skirts. The elders of the island convened, and we explained what had happened in the world since the Japanese had taken their island in 1942."

Mars Hill's William Wayne Metcalf's mother died when he was only 13, leaving his sister Myrtle to take care of the family. Metcalf lied about his age to enter the navy at age 16. He participated in the liberation of the Philippines, turning 18 in Okinawa.

David Douglas (center), pictured in Egypt, said: "I grew up in Gerton. I was on the *Frank Kellogg* with a convoy of 100 ships in the Suez preparing to launch the invasion on Sicily. I took shore leave to see the pyramids. My Dad had come out of retirement to command one of those other ships in the convoy—the *Big Foot Wallace*."

Eight Forest City boys managed to meet up aboard a transport ship en route to the European theater. From left to right are (first row) T. A. Jones, H. O. Gettys, F. E. Hubbard, and J. M. Butler; (second row) W. A. Williams, C. R. Tate, H. P. Lowdermilk Jr., and C. W. Sick. (North Carolina State Archives.)

Ralph Lewis recalls the day his boat was hit by an incoming kamikaze. One particular plane had been hit and began to fall across the deck of the ship. Lewis, 21 at the time, could see the pilot just before the plane exploded. The captain ordered the crew to abandon ship. Lewis was in the water several hours before being rescued. Others were not so lucky.

Black Mountain's John Galbreath served as a navy chaplain. His unit landed at Iwo Jima, where he spent a month ministering to the wounded and dying soldiers. During this time, he witnessed the raising of the flag on Mount Sarabachi. Dick Fiske, Eugene Blankenship, and (in rear) John Galbreath posed on Iwo Jima with Mount Sarabachi in the background.

John Berdie was stationed in the South Pacific, where he had several bouts of illness. He got dengue fever in Tacloban, Leyte, the Philippines. Later he came down with hepatitis, leaving his six-foot-tall body weighing only 120 pounds.

Madison County native Frank Hicks served aboard the USS *Bush* in the Pacific. He spent a night in the water after a kamikaze attack sank the *Bush*. He managed to signal a rescuing ship by shooting a flare gun that he grabbed just before abandoning ship.

George Clifford Crawford grew up in Black Mountain, entering the Naval Academy in 1917. At the beginning of World War II, he was serving as a special naval observer in London, England. By 1946, he was made a rear admiral. He spent his last 10 years of life back in the Asheville area. Here he is awarded the Legion of Honor aboard the USS *Aegir.* (Swannanoa Valley Museum.)

Canton was home to two Congressional Medal of Honor winners. Max Thompson (left) earned his by single-handedly driving back German troops who had overrun his platoon's division. Later that same night in October 1944, he dislodged Germans from a critical pillbox, continuing his solo attack after being wounded. William D. Halyburton Jr. (bottom) served as a pharmacist's mate with the Marine Rifle Company in the 2nd Battalion, 5th Marines, in May 1945 in the assault on Okinawa. According to his citation, in an attempt to offer first aid to wounded soldiers he "unhesitatingly dashed . . . [into] a terrific concentration of mortar, machinegun, and sniper fire." When the marine he was treating suffered a second hit, Halyburton "shielded the fallen fighter with his own body and staunchly continued his ministrations . . . until he himself sustained mortal wounds and collapsed." (Top and bottom, Canton Area Historical Museum.)

Jules Blum, second from left, grew up in Munkacs, Hungary. At 17, he was captured, badly beaten, and put on a train for Auschwitz. Of the selection process, he recalled: "I got off the train and saw a man I later knew as Dr. Joseph Mengele in front of a line of people. He was impeccably dressed. . . . He saw my [badly beaten] face and asked in German 'Can you run?' When I replied, 'Yes,' he said, 'Run,' and pointed to the left. And I ran." Blum spent the next year surviving three slave labor camps before finally being liberated from Mathausen on May 14, 1945. In 1966, Blum moved to Asheville where he opened Blue Jay Knitting Mills, a textile company.

Walter Ziffer (left), now living in Weaverville, was 12 when the Nazis rolled into Czechoslovakia and set up their offices in his family home. By age 14, he was imprisoned in a series of slave labor camps, where he worked on building part of the Autobahn, loading bombs, and drilling in sub-zero weather. Starved, beaten, and brutalized, he later asked, "What does one do after a slavery experience?"

Austrian refugee and American GI Eric Wellisch took this photograph of the approach to Buchenwald in April 1945. As the Allies began to liberate the death camps, it was difficult to comprehend what they found. Wellisch, of Asheville, recalls: "I was with Patton's Army in the engineering division. We came on Buchenwald two days after it had been liberated. It was a sight I can never forget. First it was the smell, which you could smell far, far away. When I got there I couldn't believe it—piles and piles of skeleton bodies." By the end of the war, the Nazis had murdered over 11 million people in the deportation, slave labor, and death camps. Gerald Buchanan took the lower picture when he helped liberate Dachau as part of the 9th Infantry Division.

Forest City's PFC G. H. Randall (on the left) was a member of the 6th Rangers Battalion when they rescued 500 men held in a Japanese prison camp on Luzon. Here he speaks with one of the former POWs, Pvt. H. J. Kelly of Pineola, North Carolina. (North Carolina State Archives.)

George Lamprinakos grew up in the Greek community in Asheville. The year 1945 saw him billeted in a castle. "We got up there in the turret of the castle and as far as we could see up the road was a line of German soldiers all coming to us to be captured. The last thing they wanted to do was be captured by the Russians. We set up a way to organize them—no fences, just guards. They weren't going to run away."

James Hollandsworth was an engineer rebuilding a bridge in Germany on VE Day. In a letter to his wife, he explained this photograph: "It was my first and last smoke. . . . the boys gave me an expensive cigar for the occasion. . . . we had quite a ceremony." This was his first and only cigar of the war. Note the map on the side of the truck. The sign on the map has a swastika with the word "Kaputt" written across it. (Asheville School Archives.)

Curtis J. Rice, in the photograph to the left (right) with his son, J. T., owned Anders Rice Funeral Home. During World War II, the home held numerous services for local soldiers killed overseas. J. T. Rice entered the Army Air Corps at age 18. He trained as a flight engineer and top turret gunner (bottom image, first row, far right). In England, when news broke of victory in Europe, Rice remembers, "We like to tore that place down." His crew continued flying to maintain their training, but rather than combat, they saw Britain from the air. During this time, Rice got to spend some time in the pilot's seat.

Four

AFTER THE WAR

World War II marked the beginning of the civil rights movement, just as it sounded the end of imperialism worldwide. By war's end, over 1.2 million African Americans served in the armed forces, compared with 4,000 in 1941. The NAACP used this opportunity to call for a "double V": victory at home and victory abroad. Hilde Hoffman, a Holocaust survivor and war bride, saw a "whites only" sign in downtown Asheville for the first time in 1946 and wondered if the United States was any different than Germany. African Americans, after defending the concepts of liberty and democracy, decided to no longer stand by while racism and Jim Crow limited the potential of this nation. Indeed, in 1948, President Truman ordered the military desegregated.

The GI Bill of Rights, designed to maintain the zest of the wartime economy, provided veterans the opportunity to pursue education (thus slowing their return to the workforce) and buy a home. This funding proved critical to WNC's economy. However, once again the economic impact proved more beneficial to white veterans. George Gash understood the importance of getting an education. When he applied to the black colleges on the GI Bill, he found great competition for the relatively few spots. The North Carolina University system would remain segregated until well into the 1950s. Eventually he went to barber school on the GI Bill, but he always regretted the lost opportunity for a college education.

Women found in the war an opportunity to taste a previously unknown independence. While some women were happy to leave the workforce, with the prospect of starting a family and making a job for a returning veteran, others did not want to give up the sense of accomplishment and satisfaction they found in a job well done. Beulah King, who came to Asheville in the decades following the war, recalled the difficulty of training the men who would replace her: "They did not want me to teach them anything." This response drove many women to seek equal rights to men in the workplace. Congress passed the Civil Rights Act of 1964, addressing gender, as well as racial, discrimination. This change, a generation after the end of the war, was unarguably inspired by the lessons this nation learned during World War II.

In May 1945, Lt. Walter McGuire was awarded the Bronze Star medal as an artillery liaison officer for advancing under artillery fire to reconnoiter enemy positions. McGuire, an attorney, was later transferred to the 100th Infantry Division to prosecute over 30 courts-martial of American soldiers, including two capital cases.

Barney Gray recalls his discharge from Fort Smith, Arkansas: "We had all these medals on our uniforms, but back in the U.S. it was just the same. I walked into the bus station to buy me a ticket to Virginia. I did not look for signs. I thought all that was settled now. The guy at the counter said, 'Now look, nigger, your damn place is next door. Now get!' "

Richard Jewett commanded an engineer's regiment at the end of the war, building temporary facilities for the U.S. Army within Germany. While there, he witnessed the Soviet Red Army's treatment of displaced Russians, some of whom the Nazis had brought to Germany for slave labor. "Each morning I would see groups of displaced persons being escorted down to the railroad station by MPs. Each day I found . . . about half of each group coming up to the railroad station would kill themselves rather than go back to Russia. Later we found out that Stalin would have most of them shot and the rest of them sent to Siberia."

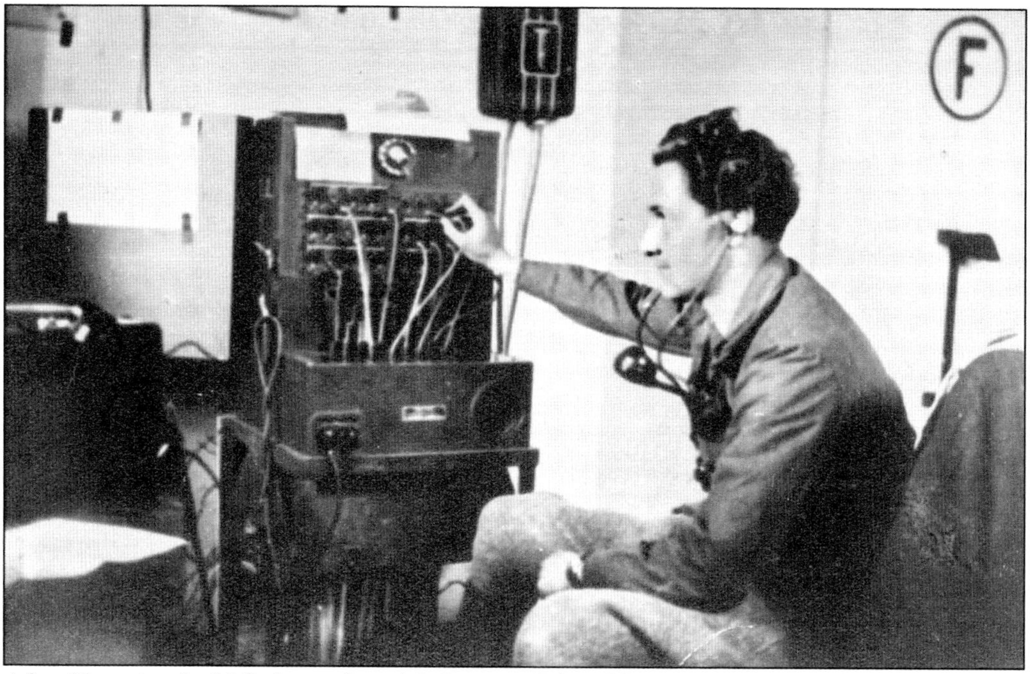

After liberation by U.S. forces from Mathausen, Julius Blum was given an identification card (below), which allowed him to travel. "This piece of paper made me human again." He worked finding homes for refugees at Leipheim Displaced Persons Camp for the United Nations Relief Agency (above) and undercover for the Israeli Haganah. In one mission, Blum posed as a soldier to rescue an orphanage of Jewish children who lost their families in the Holocaust and sent them to Palestine.

Polizeipräsident Linz/Donau Linz/Donau, den 14. MAI 1945

Bestätigung

Herr (Frau) .... geb. 30.3.25 in ....

Staatsangehörigkeit .... zuletzt wohnh. gew. ....

gibt an. Ich war im K.Z. .... von 16.5.44 bis 6.5.45

K.Z.Nr. R. 4668 .... Mein Heimatwohnort ist ....

Sonstige Angaben ....

Dokumente ....

Diese Bestätigung berechtigt zum Bezug der Lebensmittelkarten.

A.V. Obige Angaben konnten in Bezug auf die Person nicht überprüft werden.

I.A.

Der Oberbürgermeister der Gauhauptstadt Linz Ernährungsamt Abt. B

Der Polizeipräsident in Linz/Donau

During the war, as soldiers died, they were buried close to where they fell. Later the federal government offered to return each soldier to his hometown. Jesse Ray Sr. (above) worked for the Graves Registration Bureau exhuming bodies and sending them to their families. In his absence, his wife, Julia, ran the family business, Ray Funeral Home. She recalled, "Jesse was gone for one year and during that time he only came across one grave from Asheville, which he made sure was carefully returned home."

Sid Feldman (top left) faced the same task as many soldiers—getting his war bride home: "I left Asheville and Feldman's Grocery in 1942 and served in the S2 Intelligence Division in England. Our job was to brief pilots on their missions and then to debrief them when they returned. I met Terry (below) in Medmenham England where she was working in photographic intelligence, and we were married 8 months later. The government arranged for ships to bring the war brides here, but I sent her a Pan Am ticket instead. She thought I would pick her up in New York. When I wasn't there she decided to take a taxi to Asheville. Mary Morgan, the daughter of J. P. [Morgan], saw her crying, examined her ticket and told her it was for Greenville, S. C. I met her there."

Eleanor Israel and Herschel Ponder (top) married soon after the war. During the war, Eleanor had worked as a civilian for the Air Force in Asheville's City Hall. Mr. Ponder said, "The first thing I did when I got home was go duck hunting on the French Broad River. The second thing I did was go see Eleanor in Chapel Hill where she was studying." Ponder looked to square his war experiences (below) with his goals for his continuing life: "In the war I piloted a mission that I almost didn't live through. I vowed that if I lived I'd never leave home again. Later, the airlines were looking for pilots and I started to apply when I remembered my vow and decided instead to work for the railroad."

The GI Bill kept Black Mountain College's doors open for a few more years. In 1946, the college enrolled 75 students, up from a previous record of 60. By 1947, enrollment was at 90 students, over half of whom were men. (North Carolina State Archives.)

The GI Bill greatly increased enrollment for Asheville Biltmore College (now UNCA) seen here at its Merrimon Avenue location. To accommodate these students, the college bought an army surplus Quonset hut. However, in 1949, the enrollment pressure became great enough to precipitate a move to Seely's Castle on Beaucatcher Mountain. (Ball Collection, Ramsey Library, UNCA.)

Alan Neilson went to North Carolina State University on the GI Bill. He and his wife, Lucille, struggled to make it each month on the tiny allotments. More than once, Lucille would say, "If the check doesn't come tomorrow I am going to call Daddy." Alan would generally reply, "Wait one more day." Sure enough, it would arrive—for the two of them and most families on the street.

Under the leadership of Pres. Arthur Bannerman, Warren Wilson College had already taken on a good number of international students by the beginning of the war. With many European schools destroyed by the end of the war, the late 1940s and 1950s saw 20 percent of the student body comprised of international students. (Warren Wilson College Archives.)

In 1947, to help memorialize their 24 fallen alumni, the Asheville School built Memorial Hall, which served for years as a dining hall. (Asheville School Archives.)

Margaret Ensley at 18 worked as the first female laboratory technician and supervisor at Southern Dairies (seen here). She recalls: "I liked my job and my men. They treated me as their sister. . . . They taught me how to roll a ten-gallon milk can and scrub the milk stone. . . . I even picked up a few choice words of profanity." Nevertheless, Ensley readily left her job after the war so a veteran could have it. (Ball Collection, Ramsey Library, UNCA.)

Herman Popkin and his two younger brothers, Harry and Ben (top row, left to right), were stationed all over the world but would write to one another. During the war they hatched a plan: "If we survive this, let's start a summer camp." After the war, they and their wives, Rosalee, Mona, and Florence (first row from left to right), scraped together all their funds and borrowed the rest, eventually establishing Camp Blue Star in Hendersonville.

Asheville native June Lamb received medical training as part of her service in the WAVES (Women Accepted for Voluntary Emergency Service) (top). In the fall of 1950, she traveled to Japan (bottom) as an X-ray technician for the Atomic Bomb Casualty Commission. She worked on a longitudinal study examining the long-term effects of radiation exposure. While the fire and flash burns of the people and the destruction of the city were impossible to ignore, the Japanese "welcomed our being there. I kept saying to myself that that would not have happened if they had taken over our country." Complications brought about by the radioactive fallout have continued to take lives every year since 1945.

AFTERWORD

In 2002, the staff of the Center for Diversity Education and 20 dedicated volunteers interviewed well over 100 veterans and civilians. Using the methodology of *Facing History and Ourselves* (www.facinghistory.org), the volunteers collected eyewitness accounts, photographs, and primary source documents. That work was formatted into an exhibit entitled "World War II Mountain Memories: Home Front to the Frontlines," which was attended by 2,500 students and 3,000 general citizens.

Since 2003, the exhibit has traveled throughout the region to universities, schools, and libraries. Meanwhile the center has worked to archive these testimonies at the Library of Congress as part of the Veterans History Project (www.loc.gov/vets/). Through a partnership with UNCA, where the center is located, the testimonies and digitized pictures have also been archived at the Ramsey Library Special Collections Web site. There you will find an in-depth complement to this book (http://toto.lib.unca.edu/).

Some may think that the stories they share are but a glimpse of the past. Instead one should read them as hard-learned wisdom, which can help everyone face the challenges of living in our contemporary world.

The Center for Diversity Education works to increase the ways diversity is covered in the daily life of the classroom in grades K–12 and on the college level. Begun in 1995, programs at the center reach 15,000 students and teachers each year. Through the curriculum of the North Carolina Standard Course of Study, activities teach about the similarities and differences in the human story across the globe and right here in our mountain home. The center travels 10 exhibits on regional history to instigate conversations between classmates, coworkers, and citizens on diversity. To learn more call 828-232-5024 or visit (www.diversityed.org).

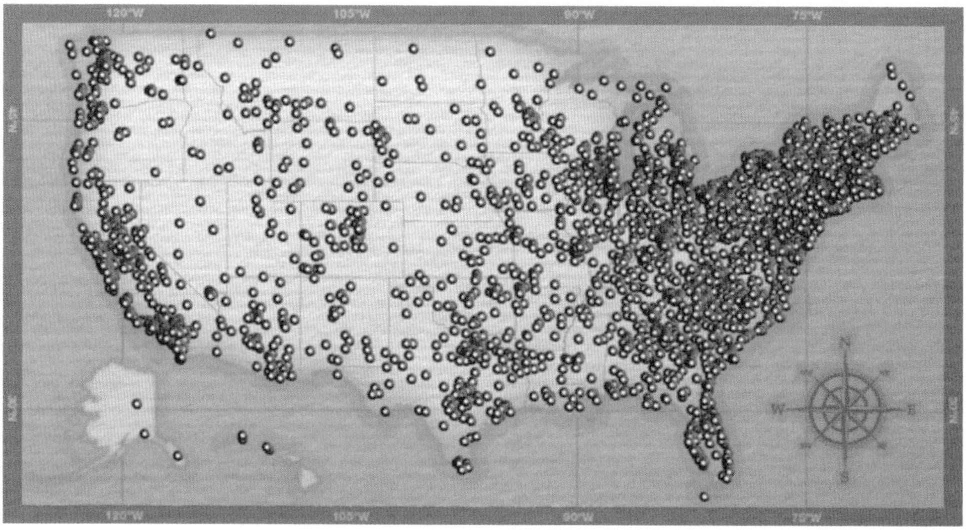